PUFFIN BOOKS

Anne Frank

THE DIARY OF A
YOUNG GIRL

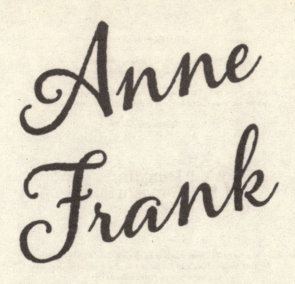

Anne Frank

THE DIARY OF A YOUNG GIRL

ABRIDGED

Based on the original writings of Anne Frank
and on the definitive edition by Mirjam Pressler

Translated by Susan Massotty

Abridged for young readers by Mirjam Pressler

Illustrations by Harry Brockway

PUFFIN

PUFFIN BOOKS

UK | USA | Canada | Ireland | Australia
India | New Zealand | South Africa

Puffin Books is part of the Penguin Random House group of companies
whose addresses can be found at global.penguinrandomhouse.com.

puffinbooks.com

Penguin
Random House
UK

The Diary of a Young Girl, Anne Frank, first published in the USA by Doubleday 1995
First published in Great Britain as a hardback by Viking and
as a paperback by Penguin Books 1997
Reprinted with further previously unpublished material by Doubleday 2001
Reprinted with further previously unpublished material by Penguin Books 2001
Published by Puffin Books 2002
This abridged edition published by Puffin Books 2015

009

Set in 12.5/17.5pt Sabon LT Std and 11.75/17.5pt Gill Sans Light by
Palimpsest Book Production Ltd, Falkirk, Stirlingshire
Printed in Great Britain by Clays Ltd, St Ives plc

A CIP catalogue record for this book is available from the British Library

ISBN: 978–0–141–34535–2

www.greenpenguin.co.uk

Introduction

Anne Frank was born on 12 June 1929 in Frankfurt am Main in Germany. The members of her family were father, Otto Frank, mother, Edith Frank (née Hollander), sister, Margot, who was three years older than Anne, and Anne herself.

Before she reached the age of four, Anne moved to Amsterdam in Holland with her family. Why? Well, the Franks were Jews and in 1933 the National Socialist Party (known as the Nazi Party) under Adolf Hitler came to power in Germany. The Nazis had two major goals: to drive the Jews, and other groups of people they believed to be inferior, out of Germany; and to gain *Lebensraum* – space to live – for the German people.

The Franks fled to Amsterdam, where Otto Frank had set up a business, which mainly sold pectin, a gelling agent used to make home-made jam.

Anne went to the Montessori nursery school, followed by the Montessori school and later attended the Jewish Lyceum.

Anne was given a diary for her thirteenth birthday. 'Maybe one of my nicest presents,' she later said. It was certainly the most important present. When the Frank family were forced into hiding from the Nazis, Anne kept her diary for two years. It was to become one of the most famous books in the world.

Mirjam Pressler

I hope I will be able to confide everything to you, as I have never been able to confide in anyone, and I hope you will be a great source of comfort and support.

This is what Anne wrote in the front of her diary on her birthday. Later, on 28 September, she added a comment:

So far you truly have been a great source of comfort to me, and so has Kitty, whom I now write to regularly. This way of keeping a diary is much nicer, and now I can hardly wait for those moments when I'm able to write in you.
Oh, I'm so glad I brought you along!

Entries in the now-famous *Diary of a Young Girl* began shortly after her thirteenth birthday.

I'll begin from the moment I got you, the moment I saw you lying on the table among my other birthday presents. (I went along when you were bought, but that doesn't count.)

On Friday, 12 June, I was awake at six o'clock, which isn't surprising, since it was my birthday. But I'm not allowed to get up at that hour, so I had to control my curiosity until quarter to seven. When I couldn't wait any longer, I went to the dining room, where Moortje (the cat) welcomed me by rubbing against my legs.

A little after seven I went to Daddy and Mummy and then to the living room to open my presents, and *you* were the first thing I saw, maybe one of my nicest presents.

Anne wrote of her other presents: flowers, a blouse, a jigsaw puzzle and books, among other things. And a birthday letter from Grammy, her grandmother on her father's side, in Basel. She took biscuits into school for her classmates and in the afternoon her friends – Hanneli Goslar, Sanne Ledermann, Ilse Wagner and Jacqueline van Maarsen – came to visit.

MONDAY, 15 JUNE 1942

I had my birthday party on Sunday afternoon. The Rin Tin Tin film was a big hit with my classmates. I got two brooches, a bookmark and two books.

Then Anne wrote about her classmates and described some of them. What follows is a small selection which shows how closely Anne watched them. It also shows that Anne already had a keen eye for detail.

Betty Bloemendaal looks rather poor, and I think she probably is. She lives on an obscure street in West Amsterdam, and none of us knows where it is. She does very well at school, but that's because she works so hard, not because she's clever. She's pretty quiet.

Jacqueline van Maarsen is supposedly my best friend, but I've never had a real friend. At first I thought Jacque would be one, but I was badly mistaken.

J.R.* – I could write a whole book about her. J. is a detestable, sneaky, stuck-up, two-faced gossip who thinks she's so grown up. She's really got Jacque under her spell, and that's a shame. J. is easily offended, bursts into tears at the slightest thing and, to top it all, is a terrible show-off. Miss J. always has to be right. She's very rich, and has a wardrobe full of the most adorable dresses that are much too old for her. She thinks she's gorgeous, but she's not. J. and I can't stand each other.

Hanneli Goslar, or Lies as she's called at school, is a bit on the strange side. She's usually shy – outspoken at home, but reserved with other people. She blabs whatever you tell her to her mother. But she says what she thinks, and lately I've come to appreciate her a great deal.

G.Z. is the prettiest girl in our class. She has a nice face, but is a bit stupid. I think they're

---

* Initials have been assigned at random to those persons who prefer to remain anonymous

going to hold her back a year, but of course I haven't told her that.

To my great surprise, G.Z. wasn't held back a year after all.

There's a lot to be said about the boys, or maybe not so much after all.

Maurice Coster is one of my many admirers, but pretty much of a pest.

Rob Cohen used to be in love with me too, but I can't stand him any more. He's an obnoxious, two-faced, lying, snivelling little twit with an awfully high opinion of himself.

Max van de Velde is a farm boy from Medemblik, but a decent sort, as Margot would say.

Albert de Mesquita came from the Montessori School and jumped a year. He's really clever.

Harry Schaap is the most decent boy in our class. He's nice.

Werner Joseph is nice too, but all the changes taking place lately have made him too quiet, so he seems boring.

Sam Salomon is one of those tough guys from the rough part of town. A real brat. (Admirer!)

Appie Riem is pretty Orthodox, but a brat too.

SATURDAY, 20 JUNE 1942

Writing in a diary is a really strange experience for someone like me. Not only because I've never written anything before, but also because it seems to me that later on neither I nor anyone else will be interested in the musings of a thirteen-year-old schoolgirl. Oh well, it doesn't matter. I feel like writing, and I have an even greater need to get all kinds of things off my chest.

'Paper has more patience than people.' I thought of this saying on one of those days when I was feeling a little depressed and was sitting at home with my chin in my hands, bored and listless, wondering whether to stay in or go out. I finally stayed where I was, brooding. Yes, paper *does* have more patience, and since I'm not planning to let anyone else read this stiff-backed notebook grandly referred to as a 'diary', unless I should ever find a real friend, it probably won't make a bit of difference.

Now I'm back to the point that prompted me to keep a diary in the first place: I don't have a friend.

Let me put it more clearly, since no one will believe that a thirteen-year-old girl is completely alone in the world. And I'm not. I have loving parents and a sixteen-year-old sister, and there are about thirty people I can call friends. I have a throng of admirers who can't keep their adoring eyes off me and who sometimes have to resort to using a broken pocket mirror to try and catch a glimpse of me in the classroom. I have a family, loving aunts and a good home. No, on the surface I seem to have everything, except my one true friend. All I think about when I'm with friends is having a good time. I can't bring myself to talk about anything but ordinary everyday things. We don't seem to be able to get any closer, and that's the problem. Maybe it's my fault that we don't confide in each other. In any case, that's just how things are, and unfortunately they're not liable to change. This is why I've started the diary.

To enhance the image of this long-awaited friend in my imagination, I don't want to jot down the facts in this diary the way most people would do, but I want the diary to be my friend, and I'm going to call this friend *Kitty*.

Since no one would understand a word of my stories to Kitty if I were to plunge right in, I'd better provide a brief sketch of my life, much as I dislike doing so.

My father, the most adorable father I've ever seen, didn't marry my mother until he was thirty-six and she was twenty-five. My sister Margot was born in Frankfurt am Main in Germany in 1926. I was born on 12 June 1929. I lived in Frankfurt until I was four. Because we're Jewish, my father emigrated to Holland in 1933, when he became the Managing Director of the Dutch Opekta Company, which manufactures products used in making jam. My mother, Edith Hollander Frank, went with him to Holland in September, while Margot and I were sent to Aachen to stay with our grandmother. Margot went to Holland in December, and I followed in February, when I was plonked down on the table as a birthday present for Margot.

I started right away at the Montessori nursery school. I stayed there until I was six, at which time I started in the first form. In the sixth form my teacher was Mrs Kuperus, the headmistress. At the end of the year we were both in tears as we said a heartbreaking farewell, because I'd been accepted at the Jewish Lyceum, where Margot also went to school.

Our lives were not without anxiety, since our relatives in Germany were suffering under Hitler's anti-Jewish laws. After the pogroms in 1938 my two uncles (my mother's brothers) fled Germany, finding safe refuge in North America. My elderly grandmother came to live with us. She was seventy-three years old at the time.

In May 1940 Germany attacked Holland. The Germans overcame the Dutch army's fierce but short-lived resistance and occupied the whole country. The war that the Nazis had started when they attacked Poland in 1939 had caught up with the Frank family and all of the German Jews who had fled to Holland. There was no escape; the borders were shut. And just as in all the other countries occupied by the Germans, anti-Jewish laws came into effect in Holland.

After May 1940 the good times were few and far between: first there was the war, then the capitulation and then the arrival of the Germans, which is when the trouble started for the Jews. Our freedom was severely restricted by a series of anti-Jewish decrees: Jews were required to wear a yellow star; Jews were required to turn in their bicycles; Jews were forbidden to use trams; Jews were forbidden to ride in cars, even their own; Jews were required to do their shopping between 3.00 and 5.00 p.m.; Jews were required to frequent only Jewish-owned barbershops and beauty salons; Jews were forbidden to be out on the streets between 8.00 p.m. and 6.00 a.m.; Jews were forbidden to go to theatres, cinemas or any other forms of entertainment; Jews were forbidden to use swimming pools, tennis courts, hockey fields or any other athletic fields; Jews were forbidden to go rowing; Jews were forbidden to take part in any athletic activity in public; Jews were forbidden to sit in their gardens or those of their friends after 8.00 p.m.; Jews were forbidden to visit Christians in their homes; Jews were required to attend Jewish schools, etc. You couldn't do this and you couldn't do that, but life went on. Jacque always said to me, 'I don't dare do anything any more, 'cause I'm afraid it's not allowed.'

In the summer of 1941 Grandma fell ill and had to have an operation, so my birthday passed with little celebration. In the summer of 1940 we didn't do much for my birthday either, since the fighting had just ended in Holland. Grandma died in January 1942. No one knows how often *I* think of her and still love her. This birthday celebration in 1942 was intended to make up for the others, and Grandma's candle was lit along with the rest.

The four of us are still doing well, and that brings me to the present date of 20 June 1942, and the solemn dedication of my diary.

SATURDAY, 20 JUNE 1942

Dearest Kitty!

Let me get started right away; it's nice and quiet now. Father and Mother are out and Margot has gone to play ping-pong with some other young people at her friend Trees's. I've been playing a lot of ping-pong myself lately. So much that five of us girls have formed a club. It's called 'The Little Dipper Minus Two'.

A really silly name, but it's based on a mistake. We wanted to give our club a special name; and because there were five of us, we came up with the idea of the Little Dipper. We thought it consisted of five stars, but we turned out to be wrong. It has seven, like the Big Dipper, which explains the 'Minus Two'. Ilse Wagner has a ping-pong set, and the Wagners let us play in their big dining room whenever we want. Since we five ping-pong players like ice-cream, especially in the summer, and since you get hot playing ping-pong, our games usually end with a visit to the nearest ice-cream parlour that allows Jews: either Oasis or Delphi. We've long since stopped hunting around for our purses or money – most of the time it's so busy in Oasis that we manage to find a few generous young men of our acquaintance or an admirer to offer us more ice-cream than we could eat in a week.

You're probably a little surprised to hear me talking about admirers at such a tender age. Unfortunately, or not, as the case may be, this vice seems to be rampant at our school. As soon as a boy asks if he can cycle home with me and we start talking, nine times out of ten I can be sure he'll become enamoured on the spot and won't let me out of his sight for a second. His ardour eventually cools, especially since I ignore his passionate glances and pedal blithely on my way. If it gets so bad that they start rambling on about 'asking Father's permission', I swerve slightly on my bike, my satchel falls, and the young man feels obliged to get off his bike and hand it to me, by which time I've switched the conversation to another topic. These are the most innocent types. Of course, there are those who blow you kisses or try to take hold of your arm, but they're definitely knocking on the wrong door. I get off my bike and either refuse to make further use of their company or act as if I'm insulted and tell them in no uncertain terms to go on home without me.

There you are. We've now laid the basis for our friendship. Until tomorrow.

Yours, Anne

Dearest Kitty,

Our entire class is quaking in its boots. The reason, of course, is the forthcoming meeting in which the teachers decide who'll move up to the next form and who'll be kept back. Half the class is making bets. If you ask me, there are so many dummies that about a quarter of the class should be kept back, but teachers are the most unpredictable creatures on earth. Maybe this time they'll be unpredictable in the right direction for a change.

I'm not so worried about my girlfriends and myself. We'll make it. The only subject I'm not sure about is maths. Anyway, all we can do is wait. Until then, we keep telling each other not to lose heart.

I get along pretty well with all my teachers. There are nine of them, seven men and two women. Mr Keesing, the old fogey who teaches maths, was annoyed with me for ages because I talked so much. After several warnings, he assigned me extra homework. An essay on the subject 'A Chatterbox'. A chatterbox, what can you write about that? I'd worry about that later,

I decided. I jotted down the title in my note-book, tucked it in my bag and tried to keep quiet.

That evening, after I'd finished the rest of my homework, the note about the essay caught my eye. I began thinking about the subject while chewing the tip of my fountain pen. Anyone could ramble on and leave big spaces between the words, but the trick was to come up with convincing arguments to prove the necessity of talking. I thought and thought, and suddenly I had an idea. I wrote the three pages Mr Keesing had assigned me and was satisfied. I argued that talking is a female trait and that I would do my best to keep it under control, but that I would never be able to cure myself of the habit, since my mother talked as much as I did, if not more, and that there's not much you can do about inherited traits.

Mr Keesing had a good laugh at my argu-ments, but when I proceeded to talk my way through the next lesson, he assigned me a second essay. This time it was supposed to be on 'An Incorrigible Chatterbox'. I handed it in, and Mr Keesing had nothing to complain about for two whole lessons. However, during the third lesson he'd finally had enough. 'Anne Frank, as punishment for talking in class, write an essay entitled "'Quack, Quack, Quack,' Said Mistress Chatterback".'

The class roared. I had to laugh too, though I'd nearly exhausted my ingenuity on the topic of chatterboxes. It was time to come up with something else, something original. My friend Sanne, who's good at poetry, offered to help me write the essay from beginning to end in verse. I jumped for joy. Keesing was trying to play a joke on me with this ridiculous subject, but I'd make sure the joke was on him.

I finished my poem, and it was beautiful! It was about a mother duck and a father swan with three baby ducklings who were bitten to death by the father because they quacked too much. Luckily, Keesing took the joke the right way. He read the poem to the class, adding his own comments, and to several other classes as well. Since then I've been allowed to talk and haven't been assigned any extra homework. On the contrary, Keesing's always making jokes these days.

Yours, Anne

Dearest Kitty,

It's sweltering. Everyone is huffing and puffing, and in this heat I have to walk everywhere. Only now do I realize how pleasant a tram is, but we Jews are no longer allowed to make use of this luxury; our own two feet are good enough for us. Yesterday at lunchtime I had an appointment with the dentist on Jan Luykenstraat. It's a long way from our school on Stadstimmertuinen. That afternoon I nearly fell asleep at my desk. Fortunately, people automatically offer you something to drink. The dental nurse is really kind.

The only mode of transport left to us is the ferry. The ferryman at Josef Israëlkade took us across when we asked him to. It's not the fault of the Dutch that we Jews are having such a bad time.

I wish I didn't have to go to school. My bike was stolen during the Easter holidays, and Father gave Mother's bike to some Christian friends for safekeeping. Thank goodness the summer holidays are almost here; one more week and our torment will be over.

Something unexpected happened yesterday morning. As I was passing the bicycle racks, I heard my name being called. I turned around and there was the nice boy I'd met the evening before at my friend Wilma's. He's Wilma's second cousin. I used to think Wilma was nice, which she is, but all she ever talks about is boys, and that gets to be a bore. He came towards me, somewhat shyly, and introduced himself as Hello Silberberg. I was a little surprised and wasn't sure what he wanted, but it didn't take me long to find out. He asked if I would allow him to accompany me to school. 'As long as you're headed that way, I'll go with you,' I said. And so we walked together. Hello is sixteen and good at telling all kinds of funny stories.

He was waiting for me again this morning, and I expect he will be from now on.

Anne

Dearest Kitty,

Until today I honestly couldn't find the time to write to you. I was with friends all day Thursday, we had company on Friday, and that's how it went until today.

Hello and I have got to know each other very well this past week, and he's told me a lot about his life. He comes from Gelsenkirchen and is living with his grandparents. His parents are in Belgium, but there's no way he can get there. Hello used to have a girlfriend named Ursula. I know her too. She's perfectly sweet and perfectly boring. Ever since he met me, Hello has realized that he's been falling asleep at Ursul's side. So I'm kind of a pep tonic. You never know what you're good for!

Then Anne wrote that Hello's grandparents were unhappy about their friendship. They thought that Anne was too young. Hello ignored them and carried on meeting Anne. Meanwhile Anne was secretly in love with another boy called Peter Schiff.

Monday evening Hello came over to meet Father and Mother. I had bought a cake and some sweets, and we had tea and biscuits, the works, but neither Hello nor I felt like sitting stiffly on our chairs. So we went out for a walk, and he didn't deliver me to my door until ten past eight. Father was furious. He said it was very wrong of me not to get home on time. I had to promise to be home by ten to eight in future. I've been asked to Hello's on Saturday.

Wilma told me that one night when Hello was at her house, she asked him, 'Who do you like best, Ursul or Anne?'

He said, 'It's none of your business.'

But as he was leaving (they hadn't talked to each other the rest of the evening), he said, 'Well, I like Anne better, but don't tell anyone. Bye!' And whoosh ... he was out of the door.

In everything he says or does, I can see that Hello is in love with me, and it's kind of nice for a change. Margot would say that Hello is a decent sort. I think so too, but he's more than that. Mother is also full of praise: 'A good-looking boy. Nice and polite.' I'm glad he's so popular with everyone. Except with my girl-friends. He thinks they're very childish, and he's right about that. Jacque still teases me about him, but I'm not in love with him. Not really. It's all right for me to have boys as friends. Nobody minds.

Mother is always asking me who I'm going to marry when I grow up, but I bet she'll never guess it's Peter, because I talked her out of that idea myself, without batting an eyelash. I love Peter as I've never loved anyone, and I tell myself he's only going around with all those other girls to hide his feelings for me. Maybe he thinks Hello and I are in love with each other, which we're not. He's just a friend, or as Mother puts it, a suitor.

Yours, Anne

SUNDAY, 5 JULY 1942

Dear Kitty,

The examination results were announced in the Jewish Theatre on Friday. My report wasn't too bad. I got one D, a C⁻ in algebra and all the rest Bs, except for two B⁺s and two B⁻s. My parents are pleased, but they're not like other parents when it comes to grades. They never worry about reports, good or bad. As long as I'm healthy and happy and not too cheeky, they're satisfied. If these three things are all right, everything else will take care of itself.

I'm just the opposite. I don't want to be a bad pupil. I was accepted at the Jewish Lyceum on a conditional basis. I was supposed to stay at the Montessori School, but when Jewish children were required to go to Jewish schools, Mr Elte finally agreed, after a great deal of persuasion, to accept Lies Goslar and me. Lies also passed this year, though she has to repeat her geometry exam.

Poor Lies. It isn't easy for her to study at home; her baby sister, a spoiled little two-year-old, plays in her room all day. If Gabi doesn't get her way, she starts screaming, and if Lies doesn't look after her, Mrs Goslar starts screaming. So Lies has a hard time doing her homework, and as long as that's the case, the extra tuition she's been getting won't help much. The Goslar household is really a sight. Mrs Goslar's parents live next door, but eat with the family. Then there's the hired help, the baby, the always absent-minded and absent Mr Goslar and the always nervous and irritable Mrs Goslar, who's expecting another baby. Lies, who's all thumbs, gets lost in the mayhem.

My sister Margot has also got her report. Brilliant, as usual. If we had such a thing as 'cum laude', she would have passed with honours, she's so clever.

Father has been home a lot lately. There's nothing for him to do at the office; it must be awful to feel you're not needed. Mr Kleiman has taken over Opekta, and Mr Kugler, Gies & Co., the company dealing in spices and spice substitutes that was set up in 1941.

One important goal for the Nazis was to seize the property and the businesses belonging to the Jews. Otto Frank got around this by transferring his company into his employees Mr Kleiman's and Mr Kugler's names.

A few days ago, as we were taking a stroll around our neighbourhood square, Father began to talk about going into hiding. He said it would be very hard for us to live cut off from the rest of the world. I asked him why he was bringing this up now.

'Well, Anne,' he replied, 'you know that for

more than a year we've been sending our clothes, food and furniture to other people. We don't want our belongings to be seized by the Germans. Nor do we want to fall into their clutches ourselves. So we'll leave of our own accord and not wait to be hauled away.'

'But when, Father?' He sounded so serious that I felt scared.

'Don't you worry. We'll take care of everything. Just enjoy your carefree life while you can.'

That was it. Oh, may these sombre words not come true for as long as possible.

The doorbell's ringing, Hello's here, time to stop.

Yours, Anne

But Anne's hopes were dashed. That same day a call-up notice arrived from the German Nazi occupiers. These call-ups told Jews to assemble in certain places at specified times in order to be taken to labour camps. At first Anne thought the call-up was for her father.

When she and I were sitting in our bedroom, Margot told me that the call-up was not for Father, but for her. At this second shock, I began to cry. Margot is sixteen – apparently they want to send girls her age away on their own. But thank goodness she won't be going; Mother had said so herself, which must be what Father had meant when he talked to me about our going into hiding. Hiding ... where would we hide? In the city? In the country? In a house? In a shack? When, where, how ...? These were questions I wasn't allowed to ask, but they still kept running through my mind.

Margot and I started packing our most important belongings into a satchel. The first thing I stuck in was this diary, and then curlers, handkerchiefs, schoolbooks, a comb and some old letters. Preoccupied by the thought of going into hiding, I stuck the craziest things in the satchel, but I'm not sorry. Memories mean more to me than dresses.

Father finally came home around five o'clock, and we rang Mr Kleiman to ask if he could come by that evening. Mr van Daan left and went to get Miep. Miep arrived and promised to return later that night, taking with her a bag full of shoes, dresses, jackets, underwear and stockings. After that it was quiet in our flat; none of us felt like eating. It was still hot, and everything was very strange.

We had rented out our big upstairs room to a Mr Goldschmidt, a divorced man in his thirties, who apparently had nothing to do that evening, since despite all our polite hints he hung around until ten o'clock.

Miep and Jan Gies came at eleven. Miep, who's worked for Father's company since 1933, has become a close friend, and so has her husband Jan. Once again, shoes, stockings, books and underwear disappeared into Miep's bag and Jan's deep pockets. At eleven thirty they too disappeared.

I was exhausted, and even though I knew it'd be my last night in my own bed, I fell asleep right away and didn't wake up until Mother called me at five thirty the next morning. Fortunately, it wasn't as hot as Sunday; a warm rain fell throughout the day. The four of us were wrapped in so many layers of clothes it looked as if we were going off to spend the night in a refrigerator, and all that just so we could take more clothes with us. No Jew in our situation would dare leave the house with a suitcase full of clothes. I was wearing two vests, three pairs of pants, a dress, and over that a skirt, a jacket, a raincoat, two pairs of stockings, heavy shoes, a cap, a scarf and lots more. I was suffocating even before we left the house, but no one bothered to ask me how I felt.

Margot stuffed her satchel with schoolbooks, went to get her bicycle and, with Miep leading the way, rode off into the great unknown. At any rate, that's how I thought of it, since I still didn't know where our hiding place was.

At seven thirty we too closed the door behind us; Moortje, my cat, was the only living creature I said goodbye to. According to a note we left for Mr Goldschmidt, she was to be taken to the neighbours, who would give her a good home.

The stripped beds, the breakfast things on the table, the pound of meat for the cat in the kitchen – all of these created the impression that we'd left in a hurry. But we weren't interested in impressions. We just wanted to get out of there, to get away and reach our destination in safety. Nothing else mattered.

More tomorrow.

Yours, Anne

THURSDAY, 9 JULY 1942

Dearest Kitty,

So there we were, Father, Mother and I, walking in the pouring rain, each of us with a satchel and a shopping bag filled to the brim with the most varied assortment of items. The people on their way to work at that early hour gave us sympathetic looks; you could tell by their faces that they were sorry they couldn't offer us some kind of transport; the conspicuous yellow star spoke for itself.

Only when we were walking down the street did Father and Mother reveal, little by little, what the plan was. For months we'd been moving as much of our furniture and apparel out of the flat as we could. It was agreed that we'd go into hiding on 16 July. Because of Margot's call-up notice, the plan had to be moved forward ten days, which meant we'd have to make do with less orderly rooms.

It was impossible to go into hiding without helpers. Helpers took care of food supplies, assisted if there were any problems, and were the only contact with the outside world. When Otto Frank decided to prepare a hiding place for his family, he asked his employees to be his helpers. Johannes Kleiman was joined by Victor Kugler, the secretary Miep Gies and Bep Voskuijl, the typist, all of whom agreed to be helpers and loyally did so for over two years. Jan Gies, Miep's husband, and Mr Voskuijl, Bep's father, who worked in the company's warehouse, should also be mentioned here. Two other warehouse assistants were not told anything about the Jews in hiding. Otto Frank's business partner, Hermann van Pels, together with his wife and their son, Peter, were going to join the Franks in their hiding place. Anne calls them the 'van Daans' in her diary.

The hiding place was located in Father's office building. That's a little hard for outsiders to understand, so I'll explain. Father didn't have a lot of people working in his office, just Mr Kugler, Mr Kleiman, Miep and a twenty-three-year-old typist named Bep Voskuijl, all of whom were informed of our coming. Mr Voskuijl, Bep's father, works in the warehouse, along with two assistants, none of whom were told anything.

Here's a description of the building. The large warehouse on the ground floor is used as a workroom and storeroom and is divided into several different sections, such as the stockroom and the milling room, where cinnamon, cloves and a pepper substitute are ground.

Next to the warehouse doors is another outside door, a separate entrance to the office. Just inside the office door is a second door, and beyond that a stairway. At the top of the stairs is another door, with a frosted window on which the word 'Office' is written in black letters. This is the big front office – very large, very light and very full. Bep, Miep and Mr Kleiman work there during the day. After passing through an alcove containing a safe, a wardrobe and a big stationery cupboard, you come to the small, dark, stuffy back office. This used to be shared by Mr Kugler and Mr van Daan, but now Mr Kugler is its only occupant. Mr Kugler's office can also be reached from the passage, but only through a glass door that can be opened from the inside but not easily from the outside. If you leave Mr Kugler's office and proceed through the long, narrow passage past the coal store and go up four steps, you find yourself in the private office, the showpiece of the entire building. Elegant mahogany furniture, a linoleum floor covered with rugs, a radio, a fancy lamp, everything first class. Next door is a spacious kitchen with a water-heater and two gas rings, and beside that a lavatory. That's the first floor.

A wooden staircase leads from the downstairs passage to the second floor. At the top of the stairs is a landing, with doors on either side. The door on the left takes you up to the spice storage area, attic and loft in the front part of the house. A typically Dutch, very steep, ankle-twisting flight of stairs also runs from the front part of the house to another door opening on to the street.

The door to the right of the landing leads to the 'Secret Annexe' at the back of the house. No one would ever suspect there were so many rooms behind that plain grey door. There's just one small step in front of the door, and then you're inside. Straight ahead of you is a steep flight of stairs. To the left is a narrow hallway opening on to a room that serves as the Frank family's living room and bedroom. Next door is a smaller room, the bedroom and study of the two young ladies of the family. To the right of the stairs is a 'bathroom', a windowless room with just a sink. The door in the corner leads to the lavatory and another one to Margot's and my room. If you go up the stairs and open the door at the top, you're surprised to see such a large, light and spacious room in an old canal-side house like this. It contains a gas cooker (thanks to the fact that it used to be Mr Kugler's laboratory) and a sink. This will be the kitchen and bedroom of Mr and Mrs van Daan, as well as the general living room, dining room and study for us all. A tiny side room is to be Peter van Daan's bedroom. Then, just as in the front part of the building, there's an attic and a loft.

Private Office

Kitchen

Bookcase

Back Office

Alcove

Front Office

1st Floor

Bed

Bed

Bed

Bed

Landing

Storeroom

Storeroom

Storeroom

2nd Floor

Folding Bed

Bed

Table

Kitchen Surface

Bed

Flat Roof

Front Attic

3rd Floor

So there you are. Now I've introduced you to the whole of our lovely Annexe!

Yours, Anne

FRIDAY, 10 JULY 1942

Dearest Kitty,

I've probably bored you with my long description of our house, but I still think you should know where I've ended up; how I ended up here is something you'll work out from my next letters.

But first, let me continue my story, because, as you know, I hadn't finished. After we arrived at 263 Prinsengracht, Miep quickly led us through the long passage and up the wooden staircase to the next floor and into the Annexe. She shut the door behind us, leaving us alone. Margot had arrived much earlier on her bike and was waiting for us.

Our living room and all the other rooms were so full of stuff that I can't find the words to describe it. All the cardboard boxes that had been sent to the office in the last few months were piled on the floors and beds. The small room was filled from floor to ceiling with linen.

If we wanted to sleep in properly made beds that night, we had to get going and tidy up the mess. Mother and Margot were unable to move a muscle. They lay down on their bare mattresses, tired, miserable and I don't know what else. But Father and I, the two cleaner-uppers in the family, started in right away.

All day long we unpacked boxes, filled cupboards, hammered nails and tidied up the mess, until we fell exhausted into our clean beds at night. We hadn't eaten a hot meal all day, but we didn't care; Mother and Margot were too tired and keyed up to eat, and Father and I were too busy.

Tuesday morning we started where we left off the night before. Bep and Miep went shopping with our ration coupons, Father worked on our blackout screens, we scrubbed the kitchen floor, and were once again busy from morning to night. Until Wednesday, I didn't have a chance to think about the enormous change in my life. Then for the first time since our arrival in the Secret Annexe, I found a moment to tell you all about it and to realize what had happened to me and what was yet to happen.

Yours, Anne

Dearest Kitty,

Father, Mother and Margot still can't get used to the chiming of the Westertoren clock, which tells us the time every quarter of an hour. Not me, I liked it from the start; it sounds so reassuring, especially at night. You no doubt want to hear what I think of being in hiding. Well, all I can say is that I don't really know yet. I don't think I'll ever feel at home in this house, but that doesn't mean I hate it. It's more like being on holiday in some strange pension. Kind of an odd way to look at life in hiding, but that's how things are. The Annexe is an ideal place to hide in. It may be damp and lopsided, but there's probably not a more comfortable hiding place in all of Amsterdam. No, in all of Holland.

Up till now our bedroom, with its blank walls, was very bare. Thanks to Father – who brought my entire postcard and film-star collection here beforehand – and to a brush and a pot of glue, I was able to plaster the walls with pictures. It looks much more cheerful. When the van Daans arrive, we'll be able to build cupboards and other odds and ends out of the wood piled in the attic.

Margot and Mother have recovered somewhat. Yesterday Mother felt well enough to cook split-pea soup for the first time, but then she was downstairs talking and forgot all about it. The beans were scorched black, and no amount of scraping could get them out of the pan.

Last night the four of us went down to the private office and listened to England on the wireless. I was so scared someone might hear it that I literally begged Father to take me back upstairs. Mother understood my anxiety and went with me. Whatever we do, we're very afraid the neighbours might hear or see us. We started off immediately the first day sewing curtains. Actually, you can hardly call them that, since they're nothing but scraps of fabric, varying greatly in shape, quality and pattern, which Father and I stitched crookedly together with unskilled fingers. These works of art were tacked to the windows, where they'll stay until we come out of hiding.

The building on our right is a branch of the Keg Company, a firm from Zaandam, and on the left is a furniture workshop. Though the people who work there are not on the premises after hours, any sound we make might travel through the walls. We've forbidden Margot to cough at night, even though she has a bad cold, and are giving her large doses of codeine.

I'm looking forward to the arrival of the van Daans, which is set for Tuesday. It will be much more fun and also not as quiet. You see, it's the silence that makes me so nervous during the evenings and nights, and I'd give anything to have one of our helpers sleep here.

It's really not that bad here, since we can do our own cooking and can listen to the wireless in Daddy's office. Mr Kleiman and Miep, and Bep Voskuijl too, have helped us so much. We've already preserved loads of rhubarb, strawberries and cherries, so for the time being I doubt we'll be bored. We also have a supply of reading material, and we're going to buy lots of games. Of course, we can't ever look out of the window or go outside. And we have to be quiet so the people downstairs can't hear us.

Yesterday we had our hands full. We had to

pit two crates of cherries for Mr Kugler to preserve. We're going to use the empty crates to make bookshelves.

Someone's calling me.

Yours, Anne

To start with, Anne saw going into hiding as a bit of an adventure. She thought it was exciting, particularly because no one knew for how long it would have to be. But soon rows broke out, on top of the general hardships.

SUNDAY, 12 JULY 1942

They were all so nice to me a month ago because of my birthday, and yet every day I feel myself drifting further away from Mother and Margot. I worked hard today and they praised me, only to start picking on me again five minutes later.

You can easily see the difference between the way they deal with Margot and the way they deal with me. For example, Margot broke the vacuum cleaner, and because of that we've been without light for the rest of the day. Mother said, 'Well, Margot, it's easy to see you're not used to working; otherwise, you'd have known better than to yank the plug out by the cord.' Margot made some reply, and that was the end of the story.

But this afternoon, when I wanted to rewrite something on Mother's shopping list because her handwriting is so hard to read, she wouldn't let me. She ticked me off again, and the whole family got involved.

I don't fit in with them, and I've felt that clearly in the last few weeks. They're so sentimental together, but I'd rather be sentimental on my own. They're always saying how nice it is with the four of us, and that we get along so well, without giving a moment's thought to the fact that I don't feel that way.

Daddy's the only one who understands me, now and again, though he usually sides with Mother and Margot. Another thing I can't stand is having them talk about me in front of outsiders, telling them how I cried or how sensibly I'm behaving. It's horrible. And sometimes they talk about Moortje and I can't bear that. Moortje is my weak spot. I miss her every minute of the day, and no one knows how often

I think of her; whenever I do, my eyes fill with tears. Moortje is so sweet, and I love her so much that I keep dreaming she'll come back to us.

I have plenty of dreams, but the reality is that we'll have to stay here until the war is over. We can't ever go outside, and the only visitors we can have are Miep, her husband Jan, Bep Voskuijl, Mr Voskuijl, Mr Kugler, Mr Kleiman and Mrs Kleiman, though she hasn't come because she thinks it's too dangerous.

FRIDAY, 14 AUGUST 1942

Dear Kitty,

I've deserted you for an entire month, but so little has happened that I can't find a newsworthy item to relate every single day. The van Daans arrived on 13 July. We thought they were coming on the fourteenth, but from the thirteenth to sixteenth the Germans were sending out call-up notices right and left and causing a lot of unrest, so they decided it would be safer to leave a day too early than a day too late.

Peter van Daan arrived at nine thirty in the morning (while we were still at breakfast). Peter's going on sixteen, a shy, awkward boy whose company won't amount to much. Mr and Mrs van Daan came half an hour later. Much to our amusement, Mrs van Daan was carrying a hatbox with a large chamber pot inside. 'I just don't feel at home without my chamber pot,' she exclaimed, and it was the first item to find a permanent place under the divan. Instead of a chamber pot, Mr van D. was lugging a collapsible tea table under his arm.

From the first, we ate our meals together, and after three days it felt as if the seven of us had become one big family. Naturally, the van Daans had much to tell about the week we'd been away from civilization. We were especially interested in what had happened to our flat and to Mr Goldschmidt.

Mr van Daan reported that people outside believed that the Frank family had found a way to flee to their relatives in Switzerland (which was a rumour the Franks themselves had spread) – supposedly an old friend of Mr Frank's, a high-ranking German officer, had offered his help.

FRIDAY, 21 AUGUST 1942

Dear Kitty,

Now our Secret Annexe has truly become secret. Because so many houses are being searched for hidden bicycles, Mr Kugler thought it would be better to have a bookcase built in front of the entrance to our hiding place. It swings out on its hinges and opens like a door. Mr Voskuijl did the carpentry work. (Mr Voskuijl has been told that the seven of us are in hiding, and he's been most helpful.)

Now whenever we want to go downstairs we have to duck and then jump. After the first three days we were all walking around with bumps on our foreheads from banging our heads against the low doorway. Then Peter cushioned it by nailing a towel stuffed with wood shavings to the door frame. Let's see if it helps!

I'm not doing much schoolwork. I've given myself a holiday until September. Father wants to start giving me lessons then, but we have to buy all the books first.

There's little change in our lives here. Peter's hair was washed today, but that's nothing special. Mr van Daan and I are always at loggerheads with each other. Mummy always treats me like a baby, which I can't stand. For the rest, things are going better. I don't think Peter's got any nicer. He's an obnoxious boy who lies around on his bed all day, only rousing himself to do a little carpentry work before returning to his nap. What a clot!

Mummy gave me another one of her dreadful sermons this morning. We take the opposite view on everything. Daddy's a sweetheart; he may get cross with me, but it never lasts longer than five minutes.

It's a beautiful day outside, nice and hot, and in spite of everything, we make the most of the weather by lounging on the folding bed in the attic.

Yours, Anne

When seven people are forced to live together in a very small space, with no work and no diversions, rows are inevitable. Anne often wrote of bickering and petty arguments, particularly between her mother and Mrs van Daan. The children were often the cause, especially Anne. Mrs van Daan thought that Mrs Frank was not strict enough with her children, that her child-rearing methods were too 'modern'.

MONDAY, 21 SEPTEMBER 1942

Dearest Kitty,

Today I'll tell you the general news here in the Annexe. A lamp has been mounted above my divan bed so that in future, when I hear the guns going off, I'll be able to pull a cord and switch on the light. I can't use it at the moment because we're keeping our window open a little, day and night.

The male members of the van Daan contingent have built a very handy wood-stained food safe, with real screens. Up till now this glorious cupboard has been located in Peter's room, but in the interests of fresh air it's been moved to the attic. Where it once stood, there's now a shelf. I advised Peter to put his table underneath the shelf, add a nice rug and hang his own cupboard where the table now stands. That might make his little cubbyhole more comfy, though I certainly wouldn't like to sleep there.

Mrs van Daan is unbearable. I'm continually being scolded for my incessant chatter when I'm upstairs. I simply let the words bounce right off me! Madame now has a new trick up her sleeve: trying to get out of washing the pots and pans. If there's a bit of food left at the bottom of the pan, she leaves it to spoil instead of transferring it to a glass dish. Then in the afternoon when Margot is stuck with cleaning all the pots and pans, Madame exclaims, 'Oh, poor Margot, you have so much work to do!'

Every other week Mr Kleiman brings me a couple of books written for girls my age. I'm enthusiastic about the *Joop ter Heul* series. I've enjoyed all of Cissy van Marxveldt's books very much. I've read *The Zaniest Summer* four times, and the ludicrous situations still make me laugh.

Father and I are currently working on our family tree, and he tells me something about each person as we go along.

I've begun my schoolwork. I'm working hard at French, cramming five irregular verbs into my head every day. But I've forgotten much too much of what I learned in school.

Peter has taken up his English with great reluctance. A few schoolbooks have just arrived, and I brought a large supply of exercise books, pencils, rubbers and labels from home. Pim (that's our pet name for Father) wants me to help him with his Dutch lessons. I'm perfectly willing to teach him in exchange for his assistance with French and other subjects. But he makes the most unbelievable mistakes!

I sometimes listen to the Dutch broadcasts from London. Prince Bernhard recently announced that Princess Juliana is expecting a baby in January, which I think is wonderful. No one here understands why I take such an interest in the Royal Family.

A few nights ago I was the topic of discussion, and we all decided I was an ignoramus. As a result, I threw myself into my schoolwork the next day, since I have little desire to still be in the first form when I'm fourteen or fifteen. The fact that I'm hardly allowed to read anything was also discussed. At the moment, Mother's reading *The House of Tavelinck*, and of course I'm not allowed to read it (though Margot is!). First I have to be more intellectually developed, like my genius of a sister. Then we discussed my ignorance of philosophy, psychology and physiology (I immediately looked up these big words in the dictionary!). It's true, I don't know anything about these subjects. But maybe I'll have learned more by next year!

I've come to the shocking conclusion that I have only one long-sleeved dress and three cardigans to wear in the winter. Father's given me permission to knit a white jumper; the wool isn't very pretty, but it'll be warm, and that's what counts. Some of our clothing was left with friends, but unfortunately we won't be able to get to it until after the war. Provided it's still there, of course.

I'd just finished writing something about Mrs van Daan when she walked into the room. Thump, I slammed the book shut.

'Hey, Anne, can't I even take a peek?'

'No, Mrs van Daan.'

'Just the last page then?'

'No, not even the last page, Mrs van Daan.'

Of course, I nearly died, since that particular page contained a rather unflattering description of her.

There's something happening every day, but I'm too tired and lazy to write it all down.

Yours, Anne

Slowly life in the Annexe settled into some kind of routine. Anne wrote of all kinds of trivial events – for example on Friday, 25 September, she wrote the following:

Some evenings I go to the van Daans for a little chat. We eat 'mothball biscuits' (biscuits that were stored in a wardrobe that was moth-proofed) and have a good time. Recently the conversation was about Peter. I said that he often pats me on the cheek, which I don't like. They asked me in a typically grown-up way whether I could ever learn to love Peter like a brother, since he loves me like a sister. 'Oh, no!' I said, but what I was thinking was, 'Oh, ugh!' Just imagine! I added that Peter's a bit stiff, perhaps because he's shy. Boys who aren't used to being around girls are like that.

At this point Anne was obviously not at all interested in Peter. When she wrote about him she only described things that she had found amusing.

SUNDAY, 27 SEPTEMBER 1942

Dearest Kitty,

Mother and I had a so-called 'discussion' today, but the annoying part is that I burst into tears. I can't help it. Daddy is *always* nice to me, and he also understands me much better. At moments like these I can't stand Mother. It's obvious that I'm a stranger to her; she doesn't even know what I think about the most ordinary things.

We were talking about maids and the fact that you're supposed to refer to them as 'domestic help' these days. She claimed that when the war is over, that's what they'll want to be called. I didn't quite see it that way. Then she added that I talk about 'later' so often and that I act as if I were such a lady, even though I'm not, but I don't think building sandcastles in the air is such a terrible thing to do, as long as you don't take it too seriously. At any rate, Daddy usually comes to my defence. Without him I wouldn't be able to stick it out here.

I don't get along with Margot very well either. Even though our family never has the same kind of outbursts they have upstairs, I find it far from pleasant. Margot's and Mother's personalities are so alien to me. I understand my girlfriends better than my own mother. Isn't that a shame?

For the umpteenth time, Mrs van Daan is sulking. She's very moody and has been removing more and more of her belongings and locking them up. It's too bad Mother doesn't repay every van Daan 'disappearing act' with a Frank 'disappearing act'.

Some people, like the van Daans, seem to take special delight not only in raising their own children but in helping others raise theirs. Margot doesn't need it, since she's naturally good, kind and clever, perfection itself, but I seem to have enough mischief for the two of us. More than once the air has been filled with the van Daans' admonitions and my cheeky replies. Father and

Mother always defend me fiercely. Without them I wouldn't be able to jump back into the fray with my usual composure. They keep telling me I should talk less, mind my own business and be more modest, but I seem doomed to failure. If Father weren't so patient, I'd have long ago given up hope of ever meeting my parents' quite moderate expectations.

If I take a small helping of a vegetable I loathe and eat potatoes instead, the van Daans, especially Mrs van Daan, can't get over how spoiled I am. 'Come on, Anne, eat some more vegetables,' she says.

'No, thank you, ma'am,' I reply. 'The potatoes are more than enough.'

'Vegetables are good for you; your mother says so too. Have some more,' she insists, until Father intervenes and upholds my right to refuse a dish I don't like.

Then Mrs van D. really flies off the handle: 'You should have been at our house, where children were brought up the way they should be. I don't call this a proper upbringing. Anne is terribly spoiled. I'd never allow that. If Anne were my daughter . . .'

This is always how her tirades begin and end: 'If Anne were my daughter . . .' Thank goodness I'm not.

But to get back to the subject of raising children, yesterday a silence fell after Mrs van D. finished her little speech. Father then replied, 'I think Anne is very well brought up. At least she's learned not to respond to your interminable sermons. As far as the vegetables are concerned, all I have to say is look who's calling the kettle black.'

Mrs van D. was soundly defeated. The pot calling the kettle black refers of course to Madame herself, since she can't tolerate beans or any kind of cabbage in the evening because they give her 'wind'. But I could say the same. What a twit, don't you think? In any case, let's hope she stops talking about me.

It's so funny to see how quickly Mrs van Daan flushes. I don't, and it secretly annoys her no end.

Yours, Anne

Dearest Kitty,

I had to stop yesterday, though I was nowhere near finished. I'm dying to tell you about another one of our clashes, but before I do I'd like to say this: I think it's odd that grown-ups quarrel so easily and so often and about such petty matters. Up till now I always thought bickering was just something children did and that they outgrew it. Of course, there's sometimes a reason to have a 'real' quarrel, but the verbal exchanges that take place here are just plain bickering. I should be used to the fact that these squabbles are daily occurrences, but I'm not and never will be as long as I'm the subject of nearly every discussion. (They refer to these as 'discussions' instead of 'quarrels', but Germans don't know the difference!) They criticize everything, and I mean everything, about me: my behaviour, my personality, my manners; every inch of me, from head to toe and back again, is the subject of gossip and debate. Harsh words and shouts are constantly being flung at my head, though I'm absolutely not used to it. According to the powers that be, I'm supposed to grin and bear it. But I can't! I have no intention of taking their insults lying down. I'll show them that Anne Frank wasn't born yesterday. They'll sit up and take notice and keep their big mouths shut when I make them see they ought to attend to their own manners instead of mine. How dare they behave like that! It's simply barbaric. I've been astonished, time and again, at such rudeness and most of all ... at such stupidity (Mrs van Daan). But as soon as I've got used to the idea, and that shouldn't take long, I'll give them a taste of their own medicine, and then they'll change their tune! Am I really as bad-mannered, headstrong, stubborn, pushy, stupid, lazy, etc., etc., as the van Daans say I am? No, of course not. I know I have my faults and shortcomings, but they blow them all out of proportion! If you only knew, Kitty, how I seethe when they scold and mock me. It won't take long before I explode with pent-up rage.

But enough of that. I've bored you long enough with my quarrels, and yet I can't resist adding a highly interesting dinner conversation.

Somehow we landed on the subject of Pim's extreme diffidence. His modesty is a well-known fact, which even the stupidest person wouldn't dream of questioning. All of a sudden Mrs van Daan, who feels the need to bring herself into every conversation, remarked, 'I'm very modest and retiring too, much more so than my husband!'

Have you ever heard anything so ridiculous? This sentence clearly illustrates that she's not exactly what you'd call modest!

Mr van Daan, who felt obliged to explain the 'much more so than my husband', answered calmly, 'I have no desire to be modest and retiring. In my experience, you get a lot further by being pushy!' And turning to me, he added, 'Don't be modest and retiring, Anne. It will get you nowhere.'

Mother agreed completely with this viewpoint. But, as usual, Mrs van Daan had to add her two penn'orth. This time, however, instead of addressing me directly, she turned to my parents and said, 'You must have a strange outlook on life to be able to say that to Anne. Things were different when I was growing up. Though they probably haven't changed much since then, except in your modern household!'

This was a direct hit at Mother's modern

child-rearing methods, which she's defended on many occasions. Mrs van Daan was so upset her face turned bright red. People who flush easily become even more agitated when they feel themselves getting hot under the collar, and they quickly lose to their opponents.

The non-flushed mother, who now wanted to have the matter over and done with as quickly as possible, paused for a moment to think before she replied. 'Well, Mrs van Daan, I agree that it's much better if a person isn't over-modest. My husband, Margot and Peter are all exceptionally modest. Your husband, Anne and I, though not exactly the opposite, don't let ourselves be pushed around.'

Mrs van Daan: 'Oh, but Mrs Frank, I don't understand what you mean! Honestly, I'm extremely modest and retiring. How can you say that I'm pushy?'

Mother: 'I didn't say you were pushy, but no one would describe you as having a retiring disposition.'

Mrs van D.: 'I'd like to know in what way I'm pushy! If I didn't look out for myself here, no one else would, and I'd soon starve, but that doesn't mean I'm not as modest and retiring as your husband.'

Mother had no choice but to laugh at this ridiculous self-defence, which irritated Mrs van Daan. Not exactly a born debater, she continued her magnificent account in a mixture of German and Dutch, until she got so tangled up in her own words that she finally rose from her chair and was just about to leave the room when her eye fell on me. You should have seen her! As luck would have it, the moment Mrs van D. turned around I was shaking my head in a combination of compassion and irony. I wasn't doing it on purpose, but I'd followed her tirade so intently that my reaction was completely involuntary. Mrs van D. wheeled around and gave me a tongue-lashing: hard, Germanic, mean and vulgar, exactly like some fat, red-faced fishwife. It was a joy to behold. If I could draw, I'd like to have sketched her as she was then. She struck me as so comical, that silly little scatterbrain! I've learned one thing: you only really get to know a person after a row. Only then can you judge their true character!

Yours, Anne

Dearest Kitty,

The strangest things happen to you when you're in hiding! Try to picture this. Because we don't have a bath, we wash ourselves in a tin tub, and because there's only hot water in the office (by which I mean the entire lower floor), the seven of us take turns making the most of this great opportunity. But since no two of us are alike and we are all plagued by varying degrees of modesty, each member of the family has selected a different place to wash. Peter takes a bath in the office kitchen, even though it has a glass door. When it's time for his bath, he goes round to each of us in turn and announces that we shouldn't walk past the kitchen for the next half-hour. He considers this measure to be sufficient. Mr van D. takes his bath upstairs, reasoning that the safety of his own room outweighs the difficulty of having to carry the hot water up all those stairs. Mrs van D. has yet to take a bath; she's waiting to see which is the best place. Father washes in the private office and Mother in the kitchen behind a fireguard, while Margot and I have declared the front office to be our bathing

59

grounds. Since the curtains are drawn on Saturday afternoon, we scrub ourselves in the dark, while the one who isn't in the bath looks out of the window through a chink in the curtains and gazes in wonder at the endlessly amusing people.

A week ago I decided I didn't like this spot and have been on the lookout for more comfortable quarters. It was Peter who gave me the idea of setting my tin bath in the spacious office lavatory. I can sit down, turn on the light, lock the door, pour out the water without anyone's help, and all without the fear of being seen. I used my lovely bathroom for the first time on Sunday and, strange as it may seem, I like it better than any other place.

The plumber was at work downstairs on Wednesday, moving the water pipes and drains from the office lavatory to the passage so the pipes won't freeze during a cold winter. The plumber's visit was far from pleasant. Not only were we not allowed to run water during the day, but the lavatory was also out of bounds. I'll tell you how we handled this problem; you may find it unseemly of me to bring it up, but I'm not so prudish about matters of this kind. On the day of our arrival, Father and I improvised a chamber pot, sacrificing a preserving jar for this purpose. For the duration of the plumber's visit, preserving jars were put into service during the daytime to hold our calls of nature. As far as I was concerned, this wasn't half as difficult as having to sit still all day and not say a word. You can imagine how hard that was for Miss Quack, Quack, Quack. On ordinary days we have to speak in a whisper; not being able to talk or move at all is ten times worse.

After three days of constant sitting, my backside was stiff and sore. Nightly callisthenics helped.

Yours, Anne

Anne wrote of all kinds of events. It had been Mrs van Daan's birthday. Bep had bought new skirts for Margot and Anne at the department store. Bep had also ordered a correspondence course in shorthand for Margot, Peter and Anne to learn shorthand. And on Thursday, 1 October, Anne wrote something nice about Peter:

From time to time Peter can be very amusing. He and I have one thing in common: we like to dress up, which makes everyone laugh. One evening we made our appearance, with Peter in one of his mother's skin-tight dresses and me in his suit. He wore a hat; I had a cap on. The grown-ups split their sides laughing, and we enjoyed ourselves every bit as much.

Bye-bye, Anne

Anne spent a lot of time daydreaming. She imagined visiting her grandmother Alice in Basel, and her aunt and uncle and cousins Stephan and Bernd (Buddy) Elias. The following list of all the things she wanted to buy showed what she was missing in the Annexe.

I imagine that . . .

I've gone to Switzerland. Daddy and I sleep in one room, while the boys' study is turned into a sitting room, where I can receive visitors. As a surprise, they've bought new furniture for me, including a tea table, a desk, armchairs and a divan. Everything's simply wonderful. After a few days Daddy gives me 150 guilders – converted into Swiss money, of course, but I'll call them guilders – and tells me to buy everything I think I'll need, all for myself. (Later on, I get a guilder a week, which I can also use to buy whatever I want.) I set off with Bernd and buy:

3 cotton vests @ 0.50 = 1.50
3 cotton knickers @ 0.50 = 1.50
3 wool vests @ 0.75 = 2.25
3 wool knickers @ 0.75 = 2.25
2 petticoats @ 0.50 = 1.00
2 bras (smallest size) @ 0.50 = 1.00
5 pyjamas @ 1.00 = 5.00
1 light dressing gown @ 2.50 = 2.50
1 thick dressing gown @ 3.00 = 3.00

2 bed jackets @ 0.75 = 1.50
1 small pillow @ 1.00 = 1.00
1 pair of lightweight slippers @ 1.00 = 1.00
1 pair of warm slippers @ 1.50 = 1.50
1 pair of summer shoes (school) @ 1.50 = 1.50
1 pair of summer shoes (best) @ 2.00 = 2.00
1 pair of winter shoes (school) @ 2.50 = 2.50
1 pair of winter shoes (best) @ 3.00 = 3.00
2 aprons @ 0.50 = 1.00
25 handkerchiefs @ 0.05 = 1.25
4 pairs of silk stockings @ 0.75 = 3.00
4 pairs of knee socks @ 0.50 = 2.00
4 pairs of socks @ 0.25 = 1.00
2 pairs of thick stockings @ 1.00 = 2.00
3 skeins of white wool (underwear, cap) = 1.50
3 skeins of blue wool (sweater, skirt) = 1.50
3 skeins of variegated wool (cap, scarf) = 1.50
Scarves, belts, collars, buttons = 1.25

Plus 2 school dresses (summer), 2 school dresses (winter), 2 good dresses (summer), 2 good dresses (winter), 1 summer skirt, 1 good winter skirt, 1 school winter skirt, 1 raincoat, 1 summer coat, 1 winter coat, 2 hats, 2 caps. For a total of 108.00 guilders.

2 handbags, 1 ice-skating outfit, 1 pair of skates, 1 case (containing powder, skin cream, foundation cream, cleansing cream, suntan lotion, cotton wool, first-aid kit, rouge, lipstick, eyebrow pencil, bath salts, bath powder, eau de Cologne, soap, powder puff).

Plus 4 sweaters @ 1.50, 4 blouses @ 1.00, miscellaneous items @ 10.00 and books, presents @ 4.50.

FRIDAY, 9 OCTOBER 1942

Dearest Kitty,

Today I have nothing but dismal and depressing news to report. Our many Jewish friends and acquaintances are being taken away in droves. The Gestapo is treating them very roughly and transporting them in cattle trucks to Westerbork, the big camp in Drenthe to which they're sending all the Jews. Miep told us about someone who'd managed to escape from there. It must be terrible in Westerbork. The people get almost nothing to eat, much less to drink, as water is available only one hour a day, and there's only one lavatory and sink for several thousand people. Men and women sleep in the same room, and women and children often have their heads shaved. Escape is almost impossible; many people look Jewish, and they're branded by their shorn heads.

If it's that bad in Holland, what must it be like in those faraway and uncivilized places where the Germans are sending them? We assume that most of them are being murdered. The English radio says they're being gassed. Perhaps that's the quickest way to die.

I feel terrible. Miep's accounts of these horrors are so heart-rending, and Miep is also very distraught. The other day, for instance, the Gestapo deposited an elderly, crippled Jewish woman on Miep's doorstep while they set off to find a car. The old woman was terrified of the glaring searchlights and the guns firing at the English planes overhead. Yet Miep didn't dare let her in. Nobody would. The Germans are generous enough when it comes to punishment.

Bep is also very subdued. Her boyfriend is being sent to Germany. Every time the planes fly over, she's afraid they're going to drop their entire bomb load on Bertus's head. Jokes like 'Oh, don't worry, they can't all fall on him' or

'One bomb is all it takes' are hardly appropriate in this situation. Bertus is not the only one being forced to work in Germany. Trainloads of young men depart daily. Some of them try to sneak off the train when it stops at a small station, but only a few manage to escape unnoticed and find a place to hide.

But that's not the end of my lamentations. Have you ever heard the term 'hostages'? That's the latest punishment for saboteurs. It's the most horrible thing you can imagine. Leading citizens – innocent people – are taken prisoner to await their execution. If the Gestapo can't find the saboteur, they simply grab five hostages and line them up against the wall. You read the announcements of their death in the paper, where they're referred to as 'fatal accidents'.

Fine specimens of humanity, those Germans, and to think I'm actually one of them! No, that's not true, Hitler took away our nationality long ago. And besides, there are no greater enemies on earth than the Germans and the Jews.

Yours, Anne

Dearest Kitty,

My hand's still shaking, though it's been two hours since we had the scare. I should explain that there are five fire extinguishers in the building. The office staff stupidly forgot to warn us that the carpenter, or whatever he's called, was coming to fill the extinguishers. As a result, we didn't bother to be quiet until I heard the sound of hammering on the landing (across from the bookcase). I immediately assumed it was the carpenter and went to warn Bep, who was eating lunch, that she couldn't go back downstairs. Father and I stationed ourselves at the door so we could hear when the man had left. After working for about fifteen minutes, he laid his hammer and some other tools on our bookcase (or so we thought!) and banged on our door. We turned white with fear. Had he heard something after all and did he now want to check out this mysterious-looking bookcase? It seemed so, since he kept knocking, pulling, pushing and jerking on it.

I was so scared I nearly fainted at the thought of this total stranger managing to discover our wonderful hiding place. Just when I thought my days were numbered, we heard Mr Kleiman's voice saying, 'Open up, it's me.'

We opened the door at once. What had happened? The hook fastening the bookcase had got stuck, which is why no one had been able to warn us about the carpenter. After the man had left, Mr Kleiman came to get Bep, but couldn't open the bookcase. I can't tell you how relieved I was. In my imagination, the man I thought was trying to get inside the Secret Annexe had kept growing and growing until he'd become not only a giant but also the cruellest fascist in the world. Whew. Fortunately, everything worked out all right, at least this time.

We had lots of fun on Monday. Miep and Jan spent the night with us. Margot and I slept in Father and Mother's room for the night so the Gieses could have our beds. The menu was drawn up in their honour, and the meal was delicious. The festivities were briefly interrupted when Father's lamp caused a short circuit and we were suddenly plunged into darkness. What were we to do? We did have fuses, but the fuse box was at the rear of the dark warehouse, which made this a particularly unpleasant job at night. Still, the men ventured forth, and ten minutes later we were able to put away the candles.

I was up early this morning. Jan was already dressed. Since he had to leave at eight thirty, he was upstairs eating breakfast by eight. Miep was busy getting dressed, and I found her in her vest when I came in. She wears the same kind of long underwear I do when she cycles. Margot and I threw on our clothes as well and were upstairs earlier than usual. After a pleasant breakfast, Miep headed downstairs. It was pouring outside and she was glad she didn't have to cycle to work. Daddy and I made the beds, and afterwards I learned five irregular French verbs. Quite industrious, don't you think?

It was hard to live in a very small space for a long time, particularly for three teenagers like Margot, Peter and Anne. They had no regular commitments, such as school, no physical exercise, and there were no diversions, such as going out or seeing friends. Margot and Anne read a lot. Anne often talked about which books she had read. Mr Kleiman borrowed books from the library again and again – pretending they were for his grandchildren – and took them instead to the Annexe.

Margot and Peter were reading in our room, with Mouschi* curled up beside Margot on the divan. After my irregular French verbs, I joined them and read *Beyond Sing the Woods*. It's quite a beautiful book, but very unusual. I'm almost finished.

Next week it's Bep's turn to spend the night.

Yours, Anne

THURSDAY, 29 OCTOBER 1942

My dearest Kitty,

I'm very worried. Father's ill. He's covered with spots and has a high temperature. It looks like measles. Just think, we can't even call a doctor! Mother is making him perspire in hopes of sweating out the fever.

---

* Peter's cat

This morning Miep told us that the furniture has been removed from the van Daans' flat on Zuider-Amstellaan. We haven't told Mrs van D. yet. She's been so *nervenmässig** lately, and we don't feel like hearing her moan and groan again about all the beautiful china and lovely chairs she had to leave behind. We had to abandon most of our nice things too. What's the good of grumbling about it now?

Father wants me to start reading books by Hebbel and other well-known German writers. I can read German fairly well by now, except that I usually mumble the words instead of reading them silently to myself. But that'll pass. Father has taken the plays of Goethe and Schiller down from the big bookcase and is planning to read to me every evening. We've started off with *Don Carlos*. Encouraged by Father's good example, Mother pressed her prayer book into my hands. I read a few prayers in German, just to be polite. They certainly sound beautiful, but they mean very little to me. Why is she making me act so religious and devout?

Tomorrow we're going to light the stove for

---

* Nervous

the first time. The chimney hasn't been swept in ages, so the room is bound to fill with smoke. Let's hope the thing draws!

Yours, Anne

Dear Kitty,

The British have finally scored a few successes in Africa and Stalingrad hasn't fallen yet, so the men are happy and we had coffee and tea this morning. For the rest, nothing special to report.

This week I've been reading a lot and doing little work. That's the way things ought to be. That's surely the road to success.

Mother and I are getting along better lately, but we're *never* close. Father's not very open about his feelings, but he's the same sweetheart he's always been. We lit the stove a few days ago and the entire room is still filled with smoke. I prefer central heating, and I'm probably not the only one. Margot's a stinker (there's no other word for it), a constant source of irritation, morning, noon and night.

Anne Frank

Dearest Kitty,

Yesterday was Peter's birthday, his sixteenth. I was upstairs by eight, and Peter and I looked at his presents. He received a game of Monopoly, a razor and a cigarette lighter. Not that he smokes so much, not at all; it just looks so distinguished.

The biggest surprise came from Mr van Daan, who reported at one that the English had landed in Tunis, Algiers, Casablanca and Oran.

'This is the beginning of the end,' everyone was saying, but Churchill, the British prime minister, who must have heard the same thing being repeated in England, declared, 'This is not the end. It is not even the beginning of the end. But it is, perhaps, the end of the beginning.' Do you see the difference? However, there's reason for optimism. Stalingrad, the Russian city that has been under attack for three months, still hasn't fallen into German hands.

In the true spirit of the Annexe, I should talk to you about food. (I should explain that they're real gluttons up on the top floor.)

Bread is delivered daily by a very nice baker,

a friend of Mr Kleiman's. Of course, we don't have as much as we did at home, but it's enough. We also purchase ration books on the black market. The price keeps going up; it's already risen from 27 to 33 guilders. And that for mere sheets of printed paper!

To provide ourselves with a source of nutrition that will keep, aside from the hundred tins of food we've stored here, we bought three hundred pounds of beans. Not just for us, but for the office staff as well. We'd hung the sacks of beans on hooks in the hallway, just inside our secret entrance, but a few seams split under the weight. So we decided to move them to the attic, and Peter was entrusted with the heavy lifting. He managed to get five of the six sacks upstairs intact and was busy with the last one when the sack broke and a flood, or rather a hailstorm, of brown beans went flying through the air and down the stairs. Since there were about fifty pounds of beans in that sack, it made enough noise to raise the dead. Downstairs they were sure the house was falling down around their heads. Peter was stunned, but then burst into peals of laughter when he saw me standing at the bottom of the stairs, like an island in a sea of brown, with waves of beans lapping at my ankles. We promptly began picking them up, but beans are so small and slippery that they roll into every conceivable corner and hole. Now each time we go upstairs, we bend over and hunt around so we can present Mrs van Daan with a handful of beans.

I almost forgot to mention that Father has recovered from his illness.

Yours, Anne

PS. The radio has just announced that Algiers has fallen. Morocco, Casablanca and Oran have been in British hands for several days. We're now waiting for Tunis.

Conditions in Holland were getting worse. Many thousands of Jews had been rounded up and sent away to concentration camps. The thinking in the Annexe was that where seven people could manage, there was room enough for eight, and if there was food enough for seven, it would do for eight. So the helpers were happy for another person to be taken into hiding – it was just as dangerous for them, whether they were helping seven people or eight. The dentist Dr Pfeffer was chosen. He had fled to Holland from Giessen in Germany, and they all knew him a little. There was no spare room left in the Annexe, so Margot, already sixteen years old, moved into her parents' room with a folding bed and Dr Pfeffer moved into her old room with Anne who, at thirteen years old, was still regarded as a child. Anne called him 'Dussel' in her diary.

TUESDAY, 17 NOVEMBER 1942

Dearest Kitty!

Mr Dussel has arrived. Everything went smoothly. Miep told him to be at a certain place in front of the post office at 11.00 a.m., when a man would meet him, and he was at the appointed place at the appointed time. Mr Kleiman went up to him, announced that the man he was expecting to meet was unable to come and asked him to drop by the office to see Miep. Mr Kleiman took a tram back to the office while Mr Dussel followed on foot.

It was eleven twenty when Mr Dussel tapped on the office door. Miep asked him to remove his coat, so the yellow star couldn't be seen, and brought him to the private office, where Mr Kleiman kept him occupied until the cleaning lady had gone. On the pretext that the private office was needed for something else, Miep took Mr Dussel upstairs, opened the bookcase and stepped inside, while Mr Dussel looked on in amazement.

In the meantime, the seven of us had seated ourselves around the dining table to await the latest addition to our family with coffee and cognac. Miep first led him into the Frank family's room. He immediately recognized our furniture, but had no idea we were upstairs, just above his head. When Miep told him, he was so astonished he nearly fainted. Thank goodness she didn't leave him in suspense any longer, but brought him upstairs. Mr Dussel sank into a chair and stared at us in dumbstruck silence, as though he thought he could read the truth on our faces. Then he stuttered, '*Aber* ... but are you *nicht* in Belgium? The officer, the auto, they were not coming? Your escape was not working?'

We explained the whole thing to him, about how we'd deliberately spread the rumour of the officer and the car to throw the Germans and anyone else who might come looking for us off the track. Mr Dussel was speechless in the face of such ingenuity, and could do nothing but gaze around in surprise as he explored the rest of our lovely and ultra-practical Annexe. We all had lunch together. Then he had a short nap, joined us for tea, put away the few belongings Miep had been able to bring here in advance and began to feel much more at home. Especially when we handed him the following typewritten rules and regulations for the Secret Annexe (a van Daan production):

PROSPECTUS AND GUIDE TO THE SECRET ANNEXE

A Unique Facility for the Temporary
Accommodation of Jews and Other
Dispossessed Persons

Open all year round: Located in beautiful, quiet, wooded surroundings in the heart of Amsterdam. No private residences in the vicinity. Can be reached by trams 13 or 17 and also by car and bicycle. For those to whom such transport has been forbidden by the German authorities, it can also be reached on foot. Furnished and unfurnished rooms and apartments are available at all times, with or without meals.

Price: Free.

Diet: Low-fat.

Running water in the bathroom (sorry, no bath) and on various inside and outside walls. Cosy stoves for heating.

Ample storage space for a variety of goods. Two large, modern safes.

Private radio with a direct line to London, New York, Tel Aviv and many other stations. Available to all residents after 6.00 p.m. No listening to forbidden broadcasts, with certain exceptions, i.e. German stations may only be tuned in to listen to classical music. It is absolutely forbidden to listen to German news bulletins (regardless of where they are transmitted from) and to pass them on to others.

Rest hours: From 10.00 p.m. to 7.30 a.m.; 10.15 a.m. on Sundays. Owing to circumstances, residents are required to observe rest hours during the daytime when instructed to do so by the Management. To ensure the safety of all, rest hours must be strictly observed!!!

Free-time activities: None allowed outside the house until further notice.

Use of language: It is necessary to speak softly

at all times. Only the language of civilized people may be spoken, thus no German.

Reading and relaxation: No German books may be read, except for the classics and works of a scholarly nature. Other books are optional.

Callisthenics: Daily.

Singing: Only softly, and after 6.00 p.m.

Films: Prior arrangements required.

Lessons: A weekly correspondence course in short-hand. Courses in English, French, maths and history offered at any hour of the day or night. Payment in the form of tuition, e.g. Dutch.

Separate department for the care of small household pets (with the exception of vermin, for which special permits are required).

Mealtimes:

Breakfast: At 9.00 a.m. daily except public holidays and Sundays; at approximately 11.30 a.m. on Sundays and public holidays.

Lunch: A light meal. From 1.15 p.m. to 1.45 p.m.

Dinner: May or may not be a hot meal. Mealtime depends on news broadcasts.

Obligations with respect to the Supply Corps: Residents must be prepared to help with office work at all times.

Baths: The tin bath is available to all residents after 9.00 a.m. on Sundays. Residents may wash in the downstairs lavatory, kitchen, private office or front office, as they choose.

Alcohol: For medicinal purposes only.

The end.

Yours, Anne

THURSDAY, 19 NOVEMBER 1942

Dearest Kitty,

Just as we thought, Mr Dussel is a very nice man. Of course he didn't mind sharing a room with me; to be honest, I'm not exactly delighted at having a stranger use my things, but you have to make sacrifices for a good cause, and I'm glad I can make this small one. 'If we can save even one of our friends, the rest doesn't matter,' said Father, and he's absolutely right.

The first day Mr Dussel was here, he asked me all sorts of questions – for example, what time the cleaning lady comes to the office, how we've arranged to use the bathroom and when we're allowed to go to the lavatory. You may laugh, but these things aren't so easy in a hiding place. During the daytime we can't make any noise that might be heard downstairs, and when someone else is there, like the cleaning lady, we have to be extra careful. I patiently explained all this to Mr Dussel, but I was surprised to see how slow he is to catch on. He asks everything twice and still can't remember what you've told him.

Maybe he's just confused by the sudden change and he'll get over it. Otherwise, everything is fine.

Mr Dussel has told us much about the outside world we've missed for so long. He had sad news. Countless friends and acquaintances have been taken off to a dreadful fate. Night after night, green and grey military vehicles cruise the streets. They knock on every door, asking whether any Jews live there. If so, the whole family is immediately taken away. If not, they proceed to the next house. It's impossible to escape their clutches unless you go into hiding. They often go around with lists, knocking only on those doors where they know there's a big haul to be made. They frequently offer a bounty, so much per head. It's like the slave hunts of the olden days. I don't mean to make light of this; it's much too tragic for that. In the evenings when it's dark, I often see long lines of good, innocent people, accompanied by crying children, walking on and on, ordered about by a handful of men who bully and beat them until they nearly drop. No one is spared. The sick, the elderly, children, babies and pregnant women – all are marched to their death.

We're so fortunate here, away from the turmoil. We wouldn't have to give a moment's thought to all this suffering if it weren't for the fact that we're so worried about those we hold dear, whom we can no longer help. I feel wicked sleeping in a warm bed, while somewhere out there my dearest friends are dropping from exhaustion or being knocked to the ground.

I get frightened myself when I think of close friends who are now at the mercy of the cruellest monsters ever to stalk the earth.

And all because they're Jews.

Yours, Anne

Dearest Kitty,

We don't really know how to react. Up till now very little news about the Jews had reached us here, and we thought it best to stay as cheerful as possible. Every now and then Miep used to mention what had happened to a friend, and Mother or Mrs van Daan would start to cry, so she decided it was better not to say any more. But we bombarded Mr Dussel with questions, and the stories he had to tell were so gruesome and dreadful that we can't get them out of our heads. Once we've had time to digest the news, we'll probably go back to our usual joking and teasing. It won't do us or those outside any good if we continue to be as gloomy as we are now. And what would be the point of turning the Secret Annexe into a Melancholy Annexe?

No matter what I'm doing, I can't help thinking about those who are gone. I catch myself laughing and remember that it's a disgrace to be so cheerful. But am I supposed to spend the whole day crying? No, I can't do that. This gloom will pass.

Added to this misery there's another, but of a more personal nature, and it pales in comparison to the suffering I've just told you about. Still, I can't help telling you that lately I've begun to feel deserted. I'm surrounded by too great a void. I never used to give it much thought, since my mind was filled with my friends and having a good time. Now I think either about unhappy things or about myself. It's taken a while, but I've finally realized that Father, no matter how kind he may be, can't take the place of my former world. When it comes to my feelings, Mother and Margot ceased to count long ago.

But why do I bother you with this foolishness? I'm terribly ungrateful, Kitty, I know, but when I've been scolded for the umpteenth time and have all these other woes to think about as well, my head begins to reel!

Yours, Anne

SATURDAY, 28 NOVEMBER 1942

Dearest Kitty,
We've been using too much electricity and have now exceeded our ration. The result: excessive economy and the prospect of having the electricity cut off. No light for a fortnight; that's

a pleasant thought, isn't it? But who knows, maybe it won't be so long! It's too dark to read after four or four thirty, so we while away the time with all kinds of crazy activities: telling riddles, doing callisthenics in the dark, speaking English or French, reviewing books – after a while everything gets boring. Yesterday I discovered a new pastime: using a good pair of binoculars to peek into the lighted rooms of the neighbours. During the day our curtains can't be opened, not even an inch, but there's no harm when it's so dark.

I never knew that neighbours could be so interesting. Ours are, at any rate. I've come across a few at dinner, one family making a cine-film and the dentist opposite working on a frightened old lady.

Mr Dussel, the man who was said to get along so well with children and to absolutely adore them, has turned out to be an old-fashioned disciplinarian and preacher of unbearably long sermons on manners. Since I have the singular pleasure (!) of sharing my far too narrow room with His Excellency, and since I'm generally considered to be the worst behaved of the three young people, it's all I can do to avoid having the same old scoldings and admonitions repeatedly flung at my head and to pretend not to hear. This wouldn't be so bad if Mr Dussel weren't such a telltale and hadn't singled out Mother to be the recipient of his reports. If Mr Dussel's just read me the Riot Act, Mother lectures me all over again, this time throwing the whole book at me. And if I'm really lucky, Mrs van D. calls me to account five minutes later and lays down the law as well!

Really, it's not easy being the badly brought-up centre of attention of a family of nit-pickers.

In bed at night, as I ponder my many sins and exaggerated shortcomings, I get so confused by the sheer amount of things I have to consider that I either laugh or cry, depending on my mood. Then I fall asleep with the strange feeling of wanting to be different from what I am or being different from what I want to be, or perhaps of behaving differently from what I am or want to be.

Oh dear, now I'm confusing you too. Forgive me, but I don't like crossing things out, and in these times of scarcity, tossing away a piece of paper is clearly taboo. So I can only advise you not to reread the above passage and to make no attempt to get to the bottom of it, because you'll never find your way out again!

Yours, Anne

Dearest Kitty,

Mr van Daan used to be in the meat, sausage and spice business. He was hired for his knowledge of spices, and yet, to our great delight, it's his sausage talents that have come in handy now.

We ordered a large amount of meat (under the counter, of course) that we were planning to preserve in case there were hard times ahead. Mr van Daan decided to make bratwurst, sausages and mettwurst. I had fun watching him put the meat through the mincer: once, twice, three times. Then he added the remaining ingredients to the minced meat and used a long pipe to force the mixture into the casings. We ate the bratwurst with sauerkraut for lunch, but the sausages, which were going to be preserved, had to dry first, so we hung them over a pole suspended from the ceiling. Everyone who came into the room burst into laughter when they saw the dangling sausages. It was such a comical sight.

The kitchen was a shambles. Mr van Daan, clad in his wife's apron and looking fatter than ever, was working away at the meat. What with his bloody hands, red face and spotted apron, he looked like a real butcher. Mrs van D. was trying to do everything at once: learning Dutch out of a book, stirring the soup, watching the meat, sighing and moaning about her broken rib. That's what happens when old (!) ladies do such stupid exercises to get rid of their fat behinds! Dussel had an eye infection and was sitting next to the stove dabbing his eye with camomile tea. Pim, seated in the one ray of sunshine coming through the window, kept having to move his chair this way and that to stay out of the way. His rheumatism must have been bothering him because he was slightly hunched over and was keeping an eye on Mr van Daan with an agonized expression on his face. He reminded me of those aged invalids you see in the poorhouse. Peter was romping around the room with Mouschi, the cat, while Mother, Margot and I were peeling boiled potatoes. When you get right down to it, none of us was doing our work properly, because we were all so busy watching Mr van Daan.

Dussel has opened his dental practice. Just for fun, I'll describe the session with his very first patient.

Mother was ironing, and Mrs van D., the first victim, sat down on a chair in the middle of the room. Dussel, unpacking his case with an air of importance, asked for some eau de Cologne, which could be used as a disinfectant, and Vaseline, which would have to do for wax. He looked in Mrs van D.'s mouth and found two teeth that made her wince with pain and utter incoherent cries every time he touched them. After a lengthy examination (lengthy as far as Mrs van D. was concerned, since it actually took no longer than two minutes), Dussel began to scrape out a cavity. But Mrs van D. had no intention of letting him. She flailed her arms and legs until Dussel finally let go of his probe and . . . it remained stuck in Mrs van D.'s tooth. That really did it! Mrs van D. lashed out wildly in all directions, cried (as much as you can with an instrument like that in your mouth), tried to remove it, but only managed to push it in even further. Mr Dussel calmly observed the scene, his hands on his hips, while the rest of the audience roared with laughter. Of course, that was very mean of us. If it'd been me, I'm sure I would have yelled even louder. After a great deal of squirming, kicking, screaming and shouting, Mrs van D. finally managed to yank the thing out, and Mr Dussel went on with his work as if nothing had happened. He was so quick that Mrs van D. didn't have time to pull any more shenanigans. But then, he had more help than he's ever had before: no fewer than two assistants; Mr van D. and I performed our job well. The whole scene resembled one of those engravings from the Middle Ages entitled 'A Quack at Work'. In the meantime, however, the patient was getting restless, since she had to keep an eye on 'her' soup and 'her' food. One thing is certain: it'll be a while before Mrs van D. makes another dental appointment!

Yours, Anne

Dearest Kitty,

I'm sitting here nice and cosy in the front office, peering out through a chink in the heavy curtains. It's dark, but there's just enough light to write by.

It's really strange watching people walk past. They all seem to be in such a hurry that they nearly trip over their own feet. Those on bicycles whizz by so fast I can't even tell who's on the bike. The people in this neighbourhood aren't particularly attractive to look at. The children especially are so dirty you wouldn't want to touch them with a bargepole. Real slum kids with runny noses. I can hardly understand a word they say.

Yesterday afternoon, when Margot and I were taking a bath, I said, 'What if we took a fishing rod and reeled in each of those kids one by one as they walked by, stuck them in the tub, washed and mended their clothes and then ...'

'And then tomorrow they'd be just as dirty and tattered as they were before,' Margot replied.

But I'm babbling. There are also other things to look at: cars, boats and the rain. I can hear the tram and the children and I'm enjoying myself.

Our thoughts are subject to as little change as we are. They're like a merry-go-round, turning from the Jews to food, from food to politics. By the way, speaking of Jews, I saw two yesterday when I was peeking through the curtains. I felt as though I were gazing at one of the Seven Wonders of the World. It gave me such a funny feeling, as if I'd denounced them to the authorities and was now spying on their misfortune.

Opposite us is a houseboat. The captain lives there with his wife and children. He has a small yapping dog. We know the little dog only by its bark and by its tail, which we can see whenever it runs round the deck. Oh, what a shame, it's just started raining and most of the people are hidden under their umbrellas. All I can see are raincoats, and now and again the back of a stocking-capped head. Actually, I don't even need to look. By now I can recognize the women at a glance: gone to fat from eating potatoes, dressed in a red or green coat and worn-out shoes, a shopping bag dangling from their arms, with faces that are either grim or good-humoured, depending on the mood of their husbands.

Yours, Anne

Dearest Kitty,

The Annexe was delighted to hear that we'll all be receiving an extra quarter of a pound of butter for Christmas. According to the newspaper, everyone is entitled to half a pound, but they mean those lucky souls who get their ration books from the government, not Jews in hiding like us who can only afford to buy four rather than eight ration books on the black market. Each of us is going to bake something with the butter. This morning I made two cakes and some biscuits. It's very busy upstairs, and Mother has informed me that I'm not to do any studying or reading until all the household tasks have been finished.

Mrs van Daan is lying in bed nursing her bruised rib. She complains all day long, constantly demands that the bandages be changed and is

95

generally dissatisfied with everything. I'll be glad when she gets back on her feet and can clean up after herself because, I must admit, she's extraordinarily hard-working and neat, and as long as she's in good physical and mental condition, she's quite cheerful.

As if I don't hear 'shh, shh' enough during the day because I'm always making 'too much' noise, my dear room-mate has come up with the idea of saying 'shh, shh' to me all night too. According to him, I shouldn't even turn over. I refuse to take any notice of him, and the next time he shushes me, I'm going to shush him right back.

He gets more exasperating and egotistical as the days go by. Except for the first week, I haven't seen even one of the biscuits he so generously promised me. He's particularly infuriating on Sundays, when he switches on the light at the crack of dawn to exercise for ten minutes.

To me, the torment seems to last for hours, since the chairs I use to make my bed longer are constantly being jiggled under my sleepy head. After rounding off his limbering-up exercises with a few vigorous arm swings, His Lordship begins dressing. His underwear is hanging on a hook, so first he lumbers over to get it and then lumbers back, past my bed. But his tie is on the table, so once again he pushes and bumps his way past the chairs.

But I mustn't waste any more of your time griping about disgusting old men. It won't help matters anyway. My plans for revenge, such as unscrewing the light bulb, locking the door and hiding his clothes, have unfortunately had to be abandoned in the interests of peace.

Oh, I'm becoming so sensible! We've got to be reasonable about everything we do here: studying, listening, holding our tongues, helping others, being kind, making compromises and I don't know what else! I'm afraid my common sense, which was in short supply to begin with, will be used up too quickly and I won't have any left by the time the war is over.

Yours, Anne

Dearest Kitty,

This morning I was constantly interrupted, and as a result I haven't been able to finish a single thing I've begun.

We have a new pastime, namely, filling packets with powdered gravy. The gravy is one of Gies & Co.'s products. Mr Kugler hasn't been able to find anyone else to fill the packets, and besides, it's cheaper if we do the job. It's the kind of work they do in prisons. It's incredibly boring and makes us dizzy and giggly.

In the meantime, the situation 'outside' had deteriorated further. Nearly one hundred thousand Jews had been arrested in Holland. Most of them were taken away to labour camps. The German occupiers also brought in food rationing. Many people suffered greatly from hunger and cold.

Terrible things are happening outside. At any time of night and day, poor helpless people are being dragged out of their homes. They're allowed to take only a rucksack and a little cash with them, and even then, they're robbed of these possessions on the way. Families are torn apart; men, women and children are separated. Children come home from school to find that their parents have disappeared. Women return from shopping to find their houses sealed, their families gone. The Christians in Holland are also living in fear because their sons are being sent to Germany. Everyone is scared. Every night hundreds of planes pass over Holland on their way to German cities, to sow their bombs on German soil. Every hour hundreds, or maybe even thousands, of people are being killed in Russia and Africa. No one can keep out of the conflict, the entire world is at war, and even though the Allies are doing better, the end is nowhere in sight.

As for us, we're quite fortunate. Luckier than millions of people. It's quiet and safe here, and we're using our money to buy food. We're so selfish that we talk about 'after the war' and look forward to new clothes and shoes, when actually we should be saving every penny to help others when the war is over, to salvage whatever we can.

The children in this neighbourhood run around in thin shirts and wooden clogs. They have no coats, no socks, no caps and no one to help them. Gnawing on a carrot to still their hunger pangs, they walk from their cold houses through cold streets to an even colder classroom. Things have got so bad in Holland that hordes of children stop passers-by in the streets to beg for a piece of bread.

I could spend hours telling you about the suffering the war has brought, but I'd only make myself more miserable. All we can do is wait, as calmly as possible, for it to end. Jews and Christians alike are waiting, the whole world is waiting, and many are waiting for death.

Yours, Anne

Dearest Kitty,

I'm seething with rage, yet I can't show it. I'd like to scream, stamp my foot, give Mother a good shaking, cry and I don't know what else because of the nasty words, mocking looks and accusations that she hurls at me day after day, piercing me like arrows from a tightly strung bow, which are nearly impossible to pull from my body. I'd like to scream at Mother, Margot, the van Daans, Dussel and Father too: 'Leave me alone, let me have at least one night when I don't cry myself to sleep with my eyes burning and my head pounding. Let me get away, away from everything, away from this world!' But I can't do that. I can't let them see my doubts, or the wounds they've inflicted on me. I couldn't bear their sympathy or their good-humoured derision. It would only make me want to scream even more.

Everyone thinks I'm showing off when I talk, ridiculous when I'm silent, insolent when I answer, cunning when I have a good idea, lazy when I'm tired, selfish when I eat one bite more than I should, stupid, cowardly, calculating, etc.,

etc. All day long I hear nothing but what an exasperating child I am, and although I laugh it off and pretend not to mind, I do mind. I wish I could ask God to give me another personality, one that doesn't antagonize everyone.

But that's impossible. I'm stuck with the character I was born with, and yet I'm sure I'm not a bad person. I do my best to please everyone, more than they'd ever suspect in a million years. When I'm upstairs, I try to laugh it off because I don't want them to see my troubles.

More than once, after a series of absurd reproaches, I've snapped at Mother: 'I don't care what you say. Why don't you just wash your hands of me – I'm a hopeless case.' Of course, she'd tell me not to talk back and virtually ignore me for two days. Then suddenly all would be forgotten and she'd treat me like everyone else.

It's impossible for me to be all smiles one day and venomous the next. I'd rather choose the golden mean, which isn't so golden, and keep my thoughts to myself. Perhaps sometime I'll treat the others with the same contempt as they treat me. Oh, if only I could.

Yours, Anne

Dearest Kitty,

Though it's been ages since I've written to you about the squabbles, there's still no change. In the beginning Mr Dussel took our soon-forgotten clashes very seriously, but now he's grown used to them and no longer tries to mediate.

Margot and Peter aren't exactly what you'd call 'young'; they're both so quiet and boring. Next to them, I stick out like a sore thumb, and I'm always being told, 'Margot and Peter don't act that way. Why don't you follow your sister's example!' I hate that.

I confess that I have absolutely no desire to be like Margot. She's too weak-willed and passive to suit me; she lets herself be swayed by others and always gives way under pressure. I want to have more backbone! But I keep ideas like these to myself. They'd only laugh at me if I offered this in my defence.

During meals the air is filled with tension. Fortunately, the outbursts are sometimes held in check by the 'soup eaters', the people from the office who come up to have a cup of soup for lunch.

This afternoon Mr van Daan again brought

up the fact that Margot eats so little. 'I suppose you do it to keep your figure,' he added in a mocking tone.

Mother, who always comes to Margot's defence, said in a loud voice, 'I can't stand that stupid chatter of yours a minute longer.'

Mrs van D. turned red as a beetroot. Mr van D. stared straight ahead and said nothing.

Still, we often have a good laugh. Not long ago Mrs van D. was entertaining us with some bit of nonsense or other. She was talking about the past, about how well she got along with her father and what a flirt he was. 'And you know,' she continued, 'my father told me that if a gentleman ever got fresh, I was to say, "Remember, sir, that I'm a lady," and he'd know what I meant.' We split our sides laughing, as if she'd told us a good joke.

Even Peter, though he's usually quiet, occasionally gives rise to hilarity. He has the misfortune of adoring foreign words without knowing what they mean. One afternoon we couldn't use the lavatory because there were visitors in the office. Unable to wait, he went to the toilet but didn't flush it. To warn us of the unpleasant smell, he tacked a sign to the door: 'RSVP – gas!' Of course, he meant 'Danger – gas!' but he thought 'RSVP' looked more elegant. He didn't have the faintest idea that it meant 'please reply'.

Yours, Anne

Dearest Kitty,

We had a short circuit last night, and besides that, the guns were booming away until dawn. I still haven't got over my fear of planes and shooting, and I crawl into Father's bed nearly every night for comfort. I know it sounds childish, but wait till it happens to you! The ack-ack guns make so much noise you can't hear your own voice. Mrs Beaverbrook,* the fatalist, practically burst into tears and said in a timid little voice, 'Oh, it's so awful. Oh, the guns are so loud!' – which is another way of saying 'I'm so scared'.

Yours, Anne

---

* A new nickname for Mrs van Daan

105

Dearest Kitty,

May I introduce: Mother Frank, the children's advocate! Extra butter for the youngsters, the problems facing today's youth – you name it, and she defends the younger generation. After a skirmish or two, she always gets her way.

One of the jars of pickled tongue has gone off. A feast for Mouschi and Boche.

You haven't met Boche yet, despite the fact that she was here before we went into hiding. She's the warehouse and office cat, who keeps the rats at bay in the storeroom. Her odd, political name can easily be explained. For a while the firm of Gies & Co. had two cats: one for the warehouse and one for the attic. Their paths crossed from time to time, which invariably resulted in a fight. The warehouse cat was always the aggressor, while the attic cat was ultimately the victor, just as in politics. So the warehouse cat was named the German, or 'Boche', and the attic cat the Englishman, or 'Tommy'. Some time after that they got rid of Tommy, but Boche is always there to amuse us when we go downstairs.

We've eaten so many brown beans and haricot beans that I can't stand to look at them. Just thinking about them makes me sick.

Our evening serving of bread has been cancelled.

Daddy just said that he's not in a very cheerful mood. His eyes look so sad again, the poor man!

I can't tear myself away from the book *A Knock at the Door* by Ina Bakker Boudier. This family saga is extremely well written, but the parts dealing with war, writers and the emancipation of women aren't very good. To be honest, these subjects don't interest me much.

Terrible bombing raids on Germany. Mr van Daan is grumpy. The reason: the cigarette shortage.

The debate about whether or not to start eating the tinned food ended in our favour.

I can't wear any of my shoes, except my ski boots, which are not very practical around the house. A pair of straw sandals that were purchased for 6.50 guilders were worn down to the soles within a week. Maybe Miep will be able to dig up something on the black market.

It's time to cut Father's hair. Pim swears that I do such a good job he'll never go to another barber after the war. If only I didn't nick his ear so often!

Yours, Anne

THURSDAY, 25 MARCH 1943

Dearest Kitty,

Mother, Father, Margot and I were sitting quite pleasantly together last night when Peter suddenly came in and whispered in Father's ear. I caught the words 'a barrel falling over in the warehouse' and 'someone fiddling with the door'.

Margot heard it too, but was trying to calm me down, since I'd turned white as chalk and was extremely nervous. The three of us waited while Father and Peter went downstairs. A minute or two later Mrs van Daan came up from where she'd been listening to the radio and told us that Pim had asked her to turn it off and tiptoe upstairs. But you know what happens when you're trying to be quiet – the old stairs creaked twice as loud. Five minutes later Peter and Pim, the colour drained from their faces, appeared again to relate their experiences.

They had positioned themselves under the staircase and waited. Nothing happened. Then all of a sudden they heard a couple of bangs, as if two doors had been slammed shut inside the house. Pim bounded up the stairs, while Peter went to warn Dussel, who finally presented himself upstairs, though not without kicking up a fuss and making a lot of noise. Then we all tiptoed in our stockinged feet to the van Daans on the next floor. Mr van D. had a bad cold and had already gone to bed, so we gathered around his bedside and discussed our suspicions in a whisper. Every time Mr van D. coughed loudly, Mrs van D. and I nearly had a nervous fit. He kept coughing until someone came up with the bright idea of giving him codeine. His cough subsided immediately.

Once again we waited and waited, but heard nothing. Finally we came to the conclusion that the burglars had taken to their heels when they heard footsteps in an otherwise quiet building. The problem now was that the chairs in the private office were neatly grouped around the radio, which was tuned to England. If the burglars had forced the door and the air-raid wardens were to notice it and call the police, there could be very serious repercussions. So Mr van Daan got up, pulled on his coat and trousers, put on his hat and cautiously followed Father down the stairs, with Peter (armed with a heavy hammer, to be on the safe side) right behind him. The ladies (including Margot and me) waited in suspense until the men returned five minutes later and reported that there was no sign of any activity in the building. We agreed not to run any water or flush the toilet; but since every-one's stomach was churning from all the tension, you can imagine the stench after we'd each had a turn in the lavatory.

Incidents like these are always accompanied by other disasters, and this was no exception. Number one: the Westertoren bells stopped chiming, and I'd always found them so comforting. Number two: Mr Voskuijl left early last night, and we weren't sure if he'd given Bep the key and she'd forgotten to lock the door.

But that was of little importance now. The night had just begun, and we still weren't sure what to expect. We were somewhat reassured by the fact that between eight fifteen – when the burglar had first entered the building and put our lives in jeopardy – and ten thirty, we hadn't heard a sound. The more we thought about it, the less likely it seemed that a burglar would have forced a door so early in the evening, when there were still people out on the streets. Besides that, it occurred to us that the warehouse manager at the Keg Company next door might still have been at work. What with the excitement and the thin walls, it's easy to mistake the sounds. Besides, your imagination often plays tricks on you in moments of danger.

So we went to bed, though not to sleep. Father and Mother and Mr Dussel were awake most of the night, and I'm not exaggerating when I say that I hardly got a wink of sleep.

This morning the men went downstairs to see if the outside door was still locked, but all was well!

Of course, we gave the entire office staff a blow-by-blow account of the incident, which had been far from pleasant. It's much easier to laugh at these kinds of things after they've happened, and Bep was the only one who took us seriously.

Yours, Anne

PS. This morning the toilet was clogged, and Father had to stick a long wooden pole and fish out several pounds of excrement and strawberry recipes (which is what we use for toilet paper these days). Afterwards we burned the pole.

SATURDAY, 27 MARCH 1943

Dearest Kitty,

We've finished our shorthand course and are now working on improving our speed. Aren't we clever! Let me tell you more about my 'time killers' (this is what I call my courses, because all we ever do is try to make the days go by as quickly as possible so we're that much closer to the end of our time here). I adore mythology, especially the Greek and Roman gods. Everyone here thinks my interest is just a passing fancy, since they've never heard of a teenager with an appreciation of mythology. Well, then, I suppose I'm the first!

Mr van Daan has a cold. Or rather, he has a scratchy throat, but he's making an enormous to-do over it. He gargles with camomile tea, coats the roof of his mouth with a tincture of myrrh and rubs Vick on his chest, nose, gums and tongue. And to top it off, he's in a foul mood!

Rauter, some German bigwig, recently gave a speech. 'All Jews must be out of the German-occupied territories before 1 July. The province of Utrecht will be cleansed of Jews [as if they were cockroaches] between 1 April and 1 May, and the provinces of North and South Holland between 1 May and 1 June.' These poor people are being shipped off to filthy slaughterhouses like a herd of sick and neglected cattle. But I'll say no more on the subject. My own thoughts give me nightmares!

One good piece of news is that the Labour Exchange was set on fire in an act of sabotage.

A few days later the Register Office also went up in flames. Men posing as German police bound and gagged the guards and managed to destroy some important documents.

Yours, Anne

SUNDAY, 2 MAY 1943

The Attitude of the Annexe Residents Towards the War

Mr van Daan. In the opinion of us all, this revered gentleman has great insight into politics. Nevertheless, he predicts we'll have to stay here until the end of '43. That's a very long time, and yet it's possible to hold out until then. But who can assure us that this war, which has caused nothing but pain and sorrow, will then be over? And that nothing will have happened to us and our helpers long before that time? No one! That's why each and every day is filled with tension. Expectation and hope generate tension, as does fear – for example, when we hear a noise inside or outside the house, when the guns go off or when we read new 'proclamations' in the paper, since we're afraid our helpers might be forced to go into hiding themselves sometime. These days everyone is talking about having to hide. We don't know how many people are actually in hiding; of course, the number is relatively small compared with the general population, but later on we'll no doubt be astonished at how many good people in Holland were willing to take Jews and Christians, with or without money, into their homes. There're also an unbelievable number of people with false identity papers.

Mrs van Daan. When this beautiful damsel (by her own account) heard that it was getting easier these days to obtain false IDs, she immediately proposed that we each have one made. As if there were nothing to it, as if Father and Mr van Daan were made of money.

Mrs van Daan is always saying the most ridiculous things, and her Putti* is often exasperated. But that's not surprising, because one day Kerli† announces, 'When this is all over, I'm going to have myself baptized'; and the next, 'As long as I can remember, I've wanted to go to Jerusalem. I only feel at home with other Jews!'

* Mrs van Daan's pet name for her husband
† Mr van Daan's pet name for his wife

Pim is a big optimist, but he always has his reasons.

Mr Dussel makes up everything as he goes along, and anyone wishing to contradict His Majesty had better think twice. In Albert Dussel's home his word is law, but that doesn't suit Anne Frank in the least.

What the other members of the Annexe family think about the war doesn't matter. When it comes to politics, these four are the only ones who count. Actually, only two of them do, but Madame van Daan and Dussel include themselves as well.

SUNDAY, 11 JULY 1943

Dear Kitty,

To get back to the subject of child-rearing (for the umpteenth time), let me tell you that I'm doing my best to be helpful, friendly and kind and to do all I can to keep the rain of rebukes down to a light drizzle. It's not easy trying to behave like a model child with people you can't stand, especially when you don't mean a word of it. But I can see that a little hypocrisy gets me a lot further than my old method of saying exactly what I think (even though no one ever asks my opinion or cares one way or another). Of course, I often forget my role and find it impossible to curb my anger when they're unfair, so that they spend the next month saying I'm the cheekiest girl in the world. Don't you think I'm to be pitied sometimes? It's a good thing I'm not a moaner, because then I might become sour and bad-tempered. I can usually see the humorous side of their scoldings, but it's easier when somebody else is being hauled over the coals.

Further, I've decided (after a great deal of thought) to drop the shorthand. First, so that I have more time for my other subjects, and second, because of my eyes. That's a sad story. I've become very short-sighted and should have had glasses ages ago. (Ugh, won't I look like a muggins!) But as you know, people in hiding can't . . .

Yesterday all anyone here could talk about was Anne's eyes, because Mother had suggested I go to the specialist with Mrs Kleiman. Just hearing this made my knees weak, since it's no small matter. Going outside! Just think of it, walking down the *street*! I can't imagine it. I was petrified at first, and then glad. But it's not as simple as all that; the various authorities who had to approve such a step were unable to reach a quick decision. They first had to carefully weigh all the difficulties and risks, though Miep was ready to set off immediately with me in tow. In the meantime, I'd taken my grey coat from the wardrobe, but it was so small it looked as if it might have belonged to my little sister. We lowered the hem, but I still couldn't button it. I'm really curious to see what they decide, only I don't think they'll ever work out a plan, because the British have landed in Sicily and Father's all set for a 'quick finish'.

Bep's been giving Margot and me a lot of office work to do. It makes us both feel important, and it's a big help to her. Anyone can file letters and make entries in a sales book, but we do it with remarkable accuracy.

Miep has so much to carry she looks like a pack mule. She goes out nearly every day in search of vegetables, and then cycles back with her purchases in large shopping bags. She's also the one who brings five library books with her every Saturday. We long for Saturdays because that means books. We're like a lot of little children with a present. Ordinary people don't know how much books can mean to someone who's cooped up. Our only diversions are reading, studying and listening to the wireless.

Yours, Anne

The Best Little Table

Yesterday afternoon Father gave me permission to ask Mr Dussel whether he would please be so good as to allow me (see how polite I am?) to use the table in our room two afternoons a week, from four to five thirty. I already sit there every day from two thirty to four while Dussel has a nap, but the rest of the time the room and the table are out of bounds to me. It's impossible to study next door in the afternoon, because there's too much going on. Besides, Father sometimes likes to sit at the desk during the afternoon.

So it seemed like a reasonable request, and I asked Dussel very politely. What do you think the learned gentleman's reply was? 'No.' Just plain 'No'!

I was incensed and wasn't about to let myself be put off like that. I asked him the reason for his 'No', but this didn't get me anywhere. The gist of his reply was: 'I have to study too, you know, and if I can't do that in the afternoons, I won't be able to fit it in at all. I have to finish the task I've set for myself; otherwise, there's no point in starting. Besides, you aren't serious about your studies. Mythology – what kind of work is that? Reading and knitting don't count either. I use that table and I'm not going to give it up!'

I replied, 'Mr Dussel, I do take my work seriously. I can't study next door in the afternoons, and I would appreciate it if you would reconsider my request!'

Having said these words, the insulted Anne turned round and pretended the learned doctor wasn't there. I was seething with rage and felt that Dussel had been incredibly rude (which he certainly had been) and that I'd been very polite.

That evening, when I managed to get hold of Pim, I told him what had happened and we discussed what my next step should be, because I had no intention of giving up and preferred to deal with the matter myself. Pim gave me a rough idea of how to approach Dussel, but cautioned me to wait until the next day, since I was in such a flap. I ignored this last piece of advice and waited for Dussel after I'd done the washing-up. Pim was sitting next door and that had a calming effect.

I began, 'Mr Dussel, you seem to believe further discussion of the matter is pointless, but I beg you to reconsider.'

Dussel gave me his most charming smile and said, 'I'm always prepared to discuss the matter, even though it's already been settled.'

I went on talking, despite Dussel's repeated interruptions. 'When you first came here,' I said, 'we agreed that the room was to be shared by the two of us. If we were to divide it fairly, you'd have the entire morning and I'd have the entire afternoon! I'm not asking for that much, but two afternoons a week does seem reasonable to me.'

Dussel leapt out of his chair as if he'd sat on a pin. 'You have no business talking about your rights to the room. Where am I supposed to go? Maybe I should ask Mr van Daan to build me a cubbyhole in the attic. You're not the only one who can't find a quiet place to work. You're always looking for a fight. If your sister Margot, who has more right to work space than you do, had come to me with the same request, I'd never even have thought of refusing, but you . . .'

And once again he brought up the business about the mythology and the knitting, and once again Anne was insulted. However, I showed no sign of it and let Dussel finish: 'But no, it's impossible to talk to you. You're shamefully self-centred. No one else matters, as long as you get your way. I've never seen such a child. But after all is said and done, I'll be obliged to let you have your way, since I don't want people saying later on that Anne Frank failed her exams because Mr Dussel refused to relinquish his table!'

He went on and on until there was such a deluge of words I could hardly keep up. For one fleeting moment I thought, 'Him and his lies. I'll smack his ugly mug so hard he'll go bouncing off the wall!' But the next moment I thought, 'Calm down, he's not worth getting so upset about!'

Margot and Anne with
their father, Otto, in 1930.

The Frank family shopping in
Frankfurt, Germany, in 1933.

Anne with her friend Sanne Ledermann,
playing outside their house on Merwedeplein,
Amsterdam, 1935.

Anne standing on the steps outside
her father's business premises, 1935.

Margot and Anne, with Grandma Hollander, on the beach at Zandvoort, a seaside resort west of Amsterdam, in the summer of 1939.

A series of studio portraits of Anne, aged 10.

Anne in her classroom at the
Montessori school in January 1940.

Anne pasted this photo into her diary and wrote,
'This is a photo as I would wish myself to look
all the time. Then I would maybe have a chance
to come to Hollywood.'

Anne sunbathing on the flat roof
of the Frank family house, 1940.

The Frank family in front of their house
on Merwedeplein, Amsterdam, 1941.

Anne, January 1941.

A portrait photo of Anne, from her
own photo album, May 1942.

Peter van Pels.
(Anne calls him Peter van Daan in her diary.)
(Date and place unknown.)

Bep Voskuijl (standing) and Miep Gies,
the office workers who helped the people
hiding in the Secret Annexe.

Johannes Kleiman, after the war, next to
the movable bookcase that concealed
the entrance to the Secret Annexe.

The rear view of Secret Annexe (top two floors and attic)
as seen from the courtyard garden.

At long last Mr Dussel's fury was spent, and he left the room with an expression of triumph mixed with wrath, his coat pockets bulging with food.

I went running over to Father and recounted the entire story, or at least those parts he hadn't been able to follow himself. Pim decided to talk to Dussel that very same evening, and they spoke for more than half an hour. They first discussed whether Anne should be allowed to use the table, yes or no. Father said that he and Dussel had dealt with the subject once before, at which time he'd professed to agree with Dussel because he didn't want to contradict the elder in front of the younger, but that, even then, he hadn't thought it was fair. Dussel felt I had no right to talk as if he were an intruder laying claim to everything in sight. But Father protested strongly, since he himself had heard me say nothing of the kind. And so the conversation went back and forth, with Father defending my 'selfishness' and my 'pointless activities' and Dussel grumbling the whole time.

Dussel finally had to give in, and I was granted the opportunity to work without interruption two afternoons a week. Dussel looked very sullen, didn't speak to me for two days and made sure he occupied the table from five to five thirty – all very childish, of course.

Anyone who's so petty and pedantic at the age of fifty-four was born that way and is never going to change.

Anne wrote about a break-in during the night, which passed unnoticed by the people hidden in the Annexe. The thieves took two cash boxes containing forty guilders and, worst of all, coupons for 330 pounds of sugar – the entire ration allowance. The people of Amsterdam were starving and it was no wonder that burglaries were increasingly common.

MONDAY, 19 JULY 1943

Dearest Kitty,

North Amsterdam was very heavily bombed on Sunday. There was apparently a great deal of destruction. Entire streets are in ruins, and it will take a while for them to dig out all the bodies. So far there have been two hundred dead and countless wounded; the hospitals are bursting at the seams. We've been told of children searching forlornly in the smouldering ruins for their dead parents. It still makes me shiver to think of the dull, distant drone that signified the approaching destruction.

Bep is currently able to get hold of exercise books, especially journals and ledgers, useful for my bookkeeping sister! Other kinds are for sale as well, but don't ask what they're like or how long they'll last. At the moment they're all labelled 'No Coupons Needed'! Like everything else you can purchase without ration stamps, they're totally worthless. They consist of twelve sheets of grey paper with narrow lines that slant across the page. Margot is thinking about taking a course in calligraphy; I've advised her to go ahead and do it. Mother won't let me because of my eyes, but I think that's silly. Whether I do that or something else, it all comes down to the same thing.

Since you've never been through a war, Kitty, and since you know very little about life in hiding, in spite of my letters, let me tell you, just for fun, what we each want to do first when we're able to go outside again.

Margot and Mr van Daan wish, above all else, to have a hot bath, filled to the brim, which they can lie in for more than half an hour. Mrs van Daan would like a cake, Dussel can think of nothing but seeing his Charlotte, and Mother is dying for a cup of real coffee. Father would like to visit Mr Voskuijl, Peter would go into town, and as for me, I'd be so overjoyed I wouldn't know where to begin.

Most of all I long to have a home of our own, to be able to move around freely and have someone help me with my homework again, at last. In other words, to go back to school!

Bep has offered to get us some fruit, at so-called bargain prices: grapes 2.50 guilders a pound, gooseberries 70 cents a pound, one peach 50 cents, melons 75 cents a pound. No wonder the papers write every evening in big, fat letters: 'Play Fair and Keep Prices Down'!

TUESDAY, 3 AUGUST 1943

Dearest Kitty,

Things are going well on the political front. Italy has banned the Fascist Party. The people are fighting the Fascists in many places – even the army has joined the fight. How can a country like that continue to wage war against England?

Our beautiful radio was taken away last week. Dussel was very angry at Mr Kugler for turning it in on the appointed day. Dussel is slipping lower and lower in my estimation, and he's already below zero. Whatever he says about politics, history, geography or anything else is so ridiculous that I hardly dare repeat it: Hitler will fade from history; the harbour in Rotterdam is bigger than the one in Hamburg; the English are idiots for not taking the opportunity to bomb Italy to smithereens; etc., etc.

We just had a third air raid. I decided to grit my teeth and practise being courageous.

Mrs van Daan, the one who always said 'Let them fall' and 'Better to end with a bang than not to end at all', is the most cowardly one among us. She was shaking like a leaf this morning and even burst into tears. She was comforted by her husband, with whom she recently declared a truce after a week of squabbling; I nearly got sentimental at the sight.

Mouschi has now proved, beyond a shadow

of a doubt, that having a cat has disadvantages as well as advantages. The whole house is crawling with fleas, and it's getting worse each day. Mr Kleiman sprinkled yellow powder in every nook and cranny, but the fleas haven't taken the slightest notice. It's making us all very jittery; we're forever imagining a bite on our arms and legs or other parts of our bodies, so we leap up and do a few exercises, since it gives us an excuse to take a better look at our arms or necks. But now we're paying the price for having had so little physical exercise; we're so stiff we can hardly turn our heads. The real callisthenics fell by the wayside long ago.

Yours, Anne

WEDNESDAY, 4 AUGUST 1943

Dearest Kitty,

Now that we've been in hiding for a little over a year, you know a great deal about our lives. Still, I can't possibly tell you everything, since it's all so different compared with ordinary times and ordinary people. Nevertheless, to give you a closer look into our lives, from time to time I'll describe part of an ordinary day. I'll start with the evening and night.

Nine in the evening. Bedtime always begins in the Annexe with an enormous hustle and bustle. Chairs are shifted, beds pulled out, blankets unfolded – nothing stays where it is during the daytime. I sleep on a small divan, which is only five feet long, so we have to add a few chairs to make it longer. Eiderdown, sheets, pillows, blankets: everything has to be removed from Dussel's bed, where it's kept during the day.

In the next room there's a terrible creaking: that's Margot's folding bed being set up. More blankets and pillows, anything to make the wooden slats a bit more comfortable. Upstairs it sounds like thunder, but it's only Mrs van D.'s bed being shoved against the window so that Her Majesty, arrayed in her pink bedjacket, can sniff the night air through her delicate little nostrils.

Nine o'clock. After Peter's finished, it's my turn for the bathroom. I wash myself from head to toe, and more often than not I find a tiny flea floating in the sink (only during the hot months, weeks or days). I brush my teeth, curl my hair, manicure my nails and dab peroxide on my upper lip to bleach the black hairs – all this in less than half an hour.

Nine thirty. I throw on my dressing gown. With soap in one hand, and potty, hairpins, knickers, curlers and cotton wool in the other, I hurry out of the bathroom. The next person in invariably calls me back to remove the gracefully curved but unsightly hairs that I've left in the sink.

Ten o'clock. Time to put up the blackout screen and say goodnight. For the next fifteen minutes, at least, the house is filled with the creaking of beds and the sigh of broken springs, and then, provided our upstairs neighbours aren't having a marital tiff in bed, all is quiet.

Eleven thirty. The bathroom door creaks. A narrow strip of light falls into the room. Squeaking shoes, a large coat, even larger than the man inside it ... Dussel is returning from his nightly work in Mr Kugler's office. I hear him shuffling back and forth for ten whole minutes, the rustle of paper (from the food he's tucking away in his cupboard) and the bed being made up. Then the figure disappears again, and the only sound is the occasional suspicious noise from the lavatory.

Approximately three o'clock. I have to get up to use the tin under my bed, which, to be on the safe side, has a rubber mat underneath in case of leaks. I always hold my breath while I go, since it clatters into the tin like a brook down a mountainside. The potty is returned to its place, and the figure in the white nightdress (the one that causes Margot to exclaim every evening, 'Oh, that indecent nightie!') climbs back into bed. A certain somebody lies awake for about fifteen minutes, listening to the sounds of the night. In the first place, to hear whether there are any burglars downstairs, and then to the various beds – upstairs, next door and in my room – to tell whether the others are asleep or half awake. This is no fun, especially when it concerns a member of the family named Dr Dussel. First, there's the sound of a fish gasping for air, and this is repeated nine or ten times. Then, the lips are moistened profusely. This is alternated with little smacking sounds, followed by a long period of tossing and turning and rearranging the pillows. After five minutes of perfect quiet, the same sequence repeats itself three more times, after which he's presumably lulled himself back to sleep for a while.

Sometimes the guns go off during the night, between one and four. I'm never aware of it before it happens, but all of a sudden I find myself standing beside my bed, out of sheer habit. Occasionally I'm dreaming so deeply (of irregular French verbs or a quarrel upstairs) that I realize only when my dream is over that the shooting has stopped and that I've remained quietly in my room. But usually I wake up. Then I grab a pillow and a handkerchief, throw on my dressing gown and slippers and dash next door to Father, just the way Margot described in this birthday poem:

When shots ring out in the dark of night,
The door creaks open and into sight
Come a hanky, a pillow, a figure in white . . .

Once I've reached the big bed, the worst is over, except when the shooting is extra loud.

Six forty-five. Brrring ... the alarm clock, which raises its shrill voice at any hour of the day or night, whether you want it to or not. Creak ... wham ... Mrs van D. turns it off. Screak ... Mr van D. gets up, puts on the water and races to the bathroom.

Seven fifteen. The door creaks again. Dussel can go to the bathroom. Alone at last, I remove the blackout screen ... and a new day begins in the Annexe.

Yours, Anne

THURSDAY, 5 AUGUST 1943

Dearest Kitty,

Today let's talk about the lunch break.

It's twelve thirty. The whole gang breathes a sigh of relief: Mr van Maaren, the man with the shady past, and Mr de Kok have gone home for lunch.

Upstairs you can hear the thud of the vacuum cleaner on Mrs van D.'s beautiful and only rug. Margot tucks a few books under her arm and heads for the class for 'slow learners', which is what Dussel seems to be. Pim goes and sits in a corner with his constant companion, Dickens, in hopes of finding a bit of peace and quiet. Mother hastens upstairs to help the busy little housewife, and I tidy up both the bathroom and myself at the same time.

Twelve forty-five. One by one they trickle in: first Mr Gies and then either Mr Kleiman or Mr Kugler, followed by Bep and sometimes even Miep.

One. Clustered round the radio, they all listen raptly to the BBC. This is the only time the members of the Annexe family don't interrupt each other, since even Mr van Daan can't argue with the speaker.

One fifteen. Food distribution. Everyone from downstairs gets a cup of soup, plus pudding, if there happens to be any. A contented Mr Gies sits on the divan or leans against the desk with his newspaper, cup and usually the cat at his side. If one of the three is missing, he doesn't hesitate to let his protest be heard. Mr Kleiman relates the latest news from town, and he's an excellent source. Mr Kugler hurries up the stairs, gives a short but solid knock on the door and comes in either wringing his hands or rubbing them in glee, depending on whether he's quiet and in a bad mood or talkative and in a good mood.

One forty-five. Everyone rises from the table and goes about their business. Margot and Mother do the washing-up, Mr and Mrs van D. head for the divan, Peter for the attic, Father for his divan, Dussel too, and Anne does her homework.

What comes next is the quietest hour of the day; when they're all asleep, there are no disturbances. To judge by his face, Dussel is dreaming of food. But I don't look at him long, because the time whizzes by and before you know it, it'll be 4.00 p.m. and the pedantic Dr Dussel will be standing with the clock in his hand because I'm one minute late clearing off the table.

Yours, Anne

MONDAY, 9 AUGUST 1943

Dearest Kitty,

We now continue with a typical day in the Annexe. Since we've already had lunch, it's time to describe dinner.

Mr van Daan. Is served first, and takes a

generous portion of whatever he likes. Usually joins in the conversation, never fails to give his opinion. Once he's spoken, his word is final. If anyone dares to suggest otherwise, Mr van D. can put up a good fight. Oh, he can hiss like a cat . . . but I'd rather he didn't. Once you've seen it, you never want to see it again. His opinion is the best, he knows the most about everything. Granted, the man has a good head on his shoulders, but it's swelled to no small degree.

Madame. Actually, the best thing would be to say nothing. Some days, especially when a foul mood is on the way, her face is hard to read. If you analyse the discussions, you realize she's not the subject, but the guilty party! A fact everyone prefers to ignore. Even so, you could call her the instigator. Stirring up trouble, now *that's* what Mrs van Daan calls fun. Stirring up trouble between Mrs Frank and Anne. Margot and Mr Frank aren't quite as easy.

But let's return to the table. Mrs van D. may think she doesn't always get enough, but that's not the case. The choicest potatoes, the tastiest morsel, the tenderest bit of whatever there is, that's Madame's motto. The others can all have their turn, as long as I get the best. (Exactly what she accuses Anne Frank of doing.) Her second watchword is: keep talking. As long as somebody's listening, it doesn't seem to occur to her to wonder whether they're interested. She must think that whatever Mrs van Daan says will interest everyone.

Smile coquettishly, pretend you know everything, offer everyone a piece of advice and mother them – that's sure to make a good impression. But if you take a better look, the good impression fades. One, she's hard-working; two, cheerful; three, coquettish – and sometimes a pretty face. That's Petronella van Daan.

The third diner. Says very little. Young Mr van Daan is usually quiet and hardly makes his presence known. As far as his appetite is concerned, he's a Danaidean vessel that never gets full. Even after the most substantial meal, he can look you calmly in the eye and claim he could have eaten twice as much.

Number four – Margot. Eats like a bird and doesn't talk at all. She eats only vegetables and fruit. 'Spoiled', in the opinion of the van Daans. 'Too little exercise and fresh air', in ours.

Beside her – Mummy. Has a hearty appetite, does her share of the talking. No one has the impression, as they do with Mrs van Daan, that this is a housewife. What's the difference between the two? Well, Mrs van D. does the cooking and Mother washes up and polishes the furniture.

Numbers six and seven. I won't say much about Father and me. The former is the most modest person at the table. He always looks to see whether the others have been served first. He needs nothing for himself; the best things are for the children. He's goodness personified. Seated next to him is the Annexe's little bundle of nerves.

Dussel. Help yourself, keep your eyes on the food, eat and don't talk. And if you have to say something, then for goodness' sake talk about food. That doesn't lead to quarrels, just to bragging. He consumes enormous portions, and 'no' is not part of his vocabulary, whether the food is good or bad.

Trousers that come up to his chest, a red jacket, black patent-leather slippers and horn-rimmed glasses – that's how he looks when he's at work at the little table, always studying and never progressing. This is interrupted only by his afternoon nap, food and – his favourite spot – the lavatory. Three, four or five times a day there's bound to be someone waiting outside the door, hopping impatiently from one foot to another, trying to hold it in and barely managing. Does Dussel care? Not a whit. From seven fifteen to seven thirty, from twelve thirty to one, from two to two fifteen, from four to four fifteen, from six to six fifteen, from eleven thirty to twelve. You can set your watch by them; these are the times for his 'regular sessions'. He never deviates or lets himself be swayed by the voices outside the door, begging him to open up before a disaster occurs.

Number nine is not part of our Annexe family, although she does share our house and table. Bep has a healthy appetite. She cleans her plate and isn't choosy. Bep's easy to please and that pleases us. She can be characterized as follows: cheerful, good-humoured, kind and willing.

A Daily Chore in Our Little Community: Peeling Potatoes!

One person goes to get some newspapers; another, the knives (keeping the best for himself, of course); the third, the potatoes; and the fourth, the water.

Mr Dussel begins. He may not always peel them very well, but he does peel non-stop, glancing left and right to see if everyone is doing it the way he does. No, they're not!

'Look, Anne, I am taking peeler in my hand like so and going from the top to bottom! *Nein*, not so . . . but so!'

'I think my way is easier, Mr Dussel,' I say tentatively.

'But this is best way, Anne. This you can take from me. Of course, it is no matter, you do the way you want.'

We go on peeling. I glance at Dussel out of the corner of my eye. Lost in thought, he shakes his head (over me, no doubt), but says no more.

I keep on peeling. Then I look at Father, on the other side of me. To Father, peeling potatoes is not a chore, but precision work. When he reads, he has a deep wrinkle in the back of his head. But when he's preparing potatoes, beans or vegetables, he seems to be totally absorbed in his task. He puts on his potato-peeling face, and when it's set in that particular way, it would be impossible for him to turn out anything less than a perfectly peeled potato.

I keep on working. I glance up for a second, but that's all the time I need. Mrs van D. is trying to attract Dussel's attention. She starts by looking in his direction, but Dussel pretends not to notice. She winks, but Dussel goes on peeling. She laughs, but Dussel still doesn't look up. Then Mother laughs too, but Dussel pays them no notice. Having failed to achieve her goal, Mrs van D. is obliged to change tactics. There's a brief silence. Then she says, 'Putti, why don't you put on an apron? Otherwise, I'll have to spend all day tomorrow trying to get the spots out of your suit!'

'I'm not getting it dirty.'

Another brief silence. 'Putti, why don't you sit down?'

'I'm fine this way. I like standing up!'

Silence.

'Putti, look out, *du spritzt schon*!'*

'I know, Mummy, but I'm being careful.'

Mrs van D. casts about for another topic. 'Um, Putti, why aren't the British carrying out any bombing raids today?'

'Because the weather's bad, Kerli!'

'But yesterday it was such nice weather and they weren't flying then either.'

'Let's drop the subject.'

'Why? Can't a person talk about that or offer an opinion?'

'No!'

'Well, why in the world not?'

'Oh, be quiet, *Mammichen*!'†

'Mr Frank always answers *his* wife.'

Mr van D. is trying to control himself. This remark always rubs him up the wrong way, but Mrs van D.'s not one to quit: 'Oh, there's never going to be an invasion!'

Mr van D. goes white, and when she notices it, Mrs van D. turns red, but she's not about to be deterred: 'The British aren't doing a thing!'

* Now you're splashing
† Mummy

The bomb bursts. 'And now shut up, *Donnerwetter noch mal*!'*

Mother can barely stifle a laugh, and I stare straight ahead.

Scenes like these are repeated almost daily, unless they've just had a terrible row. In that case, neither Mr nor Mrs van D. says a word.

It's time for me to get some more potatoes. I go up to the attic, where Peter is busy picking fleas from the cat. He looks up, the cat notices it, and whoosh . . . he's gone. Out of the window and into the rain gutter.

Peter swears; I laugh and slip out of the room.

---

* For crying out loud

Five thirty. Bep's arrival signals the beginning of our nightly freedom. Things get going right away. I go upstairs with Bep, who usually has her pudding before the rest of us. The moment she sits down, Mrs van D. begins stating her wishes. Her list usually starts with 'Oh, by the way, Bep, something else I'd like . . .' Bep winks at me. Mrs van D. doesn't miss a chance to make her wishes known to whoever comes upstairs. It must be one of the reasons none of them likes to go up there.

Five forty-five. Bep leaves. I go down two floors to have a look around: first to the kitchen, then to the private office and then to the coal store to open the cat door for Mouschi.

After a long tour of inspection, I land up in Mr Kugler's office. Mr van Daan is combing all the drawers and files for today's mail. Peter picks up Boche and the warehouse key; Pim lugs the typewriters upstairs; Margot looks around for a quiet place to do her office work; Mrs van D. puts a kettle of water on the gas ring; Mother comes down the stairs with a pan of potatoes; we all know our jobs.

Soon Peter comes back from the warehouse. The first question they ask him is whether he's remembered the bread. No, he hasn't. He crouches before the door to the front office to make himself as small as possible and crawls on his hands and knees to the steel cabinet, takes out the bread and starts to leave. At any rate, that's what he intends to do, but before he knows what's happened, Mouschi has jumped over him and gone to sit under the desk.

Peter looks all around him. Aha, there's the cat! He crawls back into the office and grabs the cat by the tail. Mouschi hisses, Peter sighs. What has he accomplished? Mouschi's now sitting by the window licking herself, very pleased at having escaped Peter's clutches. Peter has no choice but to lure her with a piece of bread. Mouschi takes the bait, follows him out, and the door closes.

I watch the entire scene through a crack in the door.

Mr van Daan is angry and slams the door. Margot and I exchange looks and think the same thing: he must have worked himself into a rage again because of some blunder on Mr Kugler's part, and he's forgotten all about the Keg Company next door.

Another step is heard in the passage. Dussel comes in, goes towards the window with an air of propriety, sniffs . . . coughs, sneezes and clears his throat. He's out of luck – it was pepper. He continues to the front office. The curtains are open, which means he can't get at his writing paper. He disappears with a scowl.

Margot and I exchange another glance. 'One less page for his sweetheart tomorrow,' I hear her say. I nod in agreement.

An elephant's tread is heard on the stairway. It's Dussel, seeking comfort in his favourite spot.

We continue working. Knock, knock, knock . . . Three taps means dinnertime!

MONDAY, 23 AUGUST 1943

Wenn Die Uhr Halb Neune Schlägt . . .*

Margot and Mother are nervous. 'Shh . . . Father. Be quiet, Otto. Shh . . . Pim! It's eight thirty. Come here, you can't run the water any more.

---

* When the clock strikes half past eight

Walk softly!' A sample of what's said to Father in the bathroom. At the stroke of half past eight, he has to be in the living room. No running water, no flushing toilet, no walking around, no noise whatsoever. As long as the office staff haven't arrived, sounds travel more easily to the warehouse.

The door opens upstairs at eight twenty, and this is followed by three gentle taps on the floor . . . Anne's porridge. I clamber up the stairs to get my dog bowl.

Back downstairs, everything has to be done quickly, quickly: I comb my hair, put away the potty, shove the bed back in place. Quiet! The clock is striking eight thirty! Mrs van D. changes her shoes and shuffles through the room in her slippers; Mr van D. too – a veritable Charlie Chaplin. All is quiet.

The ideal family scene has now reached its high point. I want to read or study and Margot does too. Father and Mother ditto. Father is sitting (with Dickens and the dictionary, of course) on the edge of the sagging, squeaky bed, which doesn't even have a decent mattress. Two bolsters can be piled on top of each other. 'I don't need these,' he thinks. 'I can manage without them!'

Once he starts reading, he doesn't look up. He laughs now and then and tries to get Mother to read a passage.

'I don't have the time right now!'

He looks disappointed, but then continues to read. A little while later, when he comes across another interesting bit, he tries again: 'You *have* to read this, Mother!'

Mother sits on the folding bed, either reading, sewing, knitting or studying, whichever is next on her list. An idea suddenly occurs to her, and she quickly says, so as not to forget, 'Anne, remember to ... Margot, jot this down ...'

After a while it's quiet again. Margot slams her book shut; Father knits his forehead, his eyebrows forming a funny curve and his wrinkle of concentration reappearing at the back of his head, and he buries himself in his book again; Mother starts chatting with Margot; and I get curious and listen too. Pim is drawn into the conversation ... Nine o'clock. Breakfast!

Dearest Kitty,

Every time I write to you, something special has happened, usually unpleasant rather than pleasant. This time, however, something wonderful is going on.

On Wednesday, 8 September, we were listening to the seven o'clock news when we heard an announcement: 'Here is some of the best news of the war so far: Italy has capitulated.' Italy has unconditionally surrendered! The Dutch broadcast from England began at eight fifteen with the news: 'Listeners, an hour and fifteen minutes ago, just as I finished writing my daily report, we received the wonderful news of Italy's capitulation. I tell you, I never tossed my notes into the wastepaper basket with more delight than I did today!'

'God Save the King', the American national anthem and the Russian 'Internationale' were played. As always, the Dutch programme was uplifting without being too optimistic.

The British have landed in Naples. Northern Italy is occupied by the Germans. The truce was signed on Friday, 3 September, the day the British landed in Italy. The Germans are ranting and raving in all the newspapers at the treachery of Badoglio and the Italian king.

Still, there's bad news as well. It's about Mr Kleiman. As you know, we all like him very much. He's unfailingly cheerful and amazingly brave, despite the fact that he's always ill and in pain and can't eat much or do a lot of walking. 'When Mr Kleiman enters a room, the sun begins to shine,' Mother said recently, and she's absolutely right.

Now it seems he has to go into hospital for a very difficult operation on his stomach, and will have to stay there for at least four weeks. You should have seen him when he said goodbye to us. He acted so normally, as though he were just off to run an errand.

Yours, Anne

THURSDAY, 16 SEPTEMBER 1943

Dearest Kitty,

Relationships here in the Annexe are getting worse all the time. We don't dare open our mouths at mealtime (except to slip in a bite of food), because no matter what we say, someone is bound to resent it or take it the wrong way.

I've been taking valerian every day to fight the anxiety and depression, but it doesn't stop me from being even more miserable the next day. A good hearty laugh would help more than ten valerian drops, but we've almost forgotten how to laugh. Sometimes I'm afraid my face is going to sag with all this sorrow and that my mouth is going to permanently droop at the corners. The others aren't doing any better. Everyone here is dreading the great terror known as winter.

SUNDAY, 17 OCTOBER 1943

Dearest Kitty,

Mr Kleiman is back, thank goodness! He looks a bit pale, and yet he cheerfully set off to sell some clothes for Mr van Daan.

The disagreeable fact is that Mr van Daan has run out of money. Mrs van D. has piles of dresses, coats and shoes, none of which she feels she can do without. Mr van D.'s suit is difficult to shift, and Peter's bike was put up for sale but is back again, since nobody wanted it. But the story doesn't end there. You see, Mrs van D. is going to have to part with her fur coat. In her opinion, the firm should pay for our upkeep, but that's ridiculous. They just had a flaming row about it and have entered the 'oh, my sweet Putti' and 'darling Kerli' stage of reconciliation.

My mind boggles at the profanity this honourable house has had to endure in the past month. Father walks around with his lips pressed together, and whenever he hears his name, he looks up in alarm, as if he's afraid he'll be called upon to resolve another delicate problem. Mother's so overwrought her cheeks are blotched with red, Margot complains of headaches, Dussel can't sleep, Mrs van D. frets and fumes all day long, and I've gone completely round the bend. To tell you the truth, I sometimes forget who we're at odds with and who we're not.

The only way to take my mind off it is to study, and I've been doing a lot of that lately.

Yours, Anne

Dearest Kitty,

Mother's nerves are very much on edge, and that doesn't bode well for me. Is it just a coincidence that Father and Mother never scold Margot and always blame me for everything? Last night, for example, Margot was reading a book with beautiful illustrations; she got up and put the book aside for later. I wasn't doing anything, so I picked it up and began looking at the pictures. Margot came back, saw 'her' book in my hands, knitted her brow and crossly demanded the book back. I wanted to look through it a bit more. Margot got angrier by the minute, and Mother butted in: 'Margot was reading that book; give it back to her.'

Father came in, and without even knowing what was going on, saw that Margot was being wronged and lashed out at me: 'I'd like to see what you'd do if Margot was looking at one of your books!'

I promptly gave in, put the book down and, according to them, left the room 'in a huff'. I was neither huffy nor cross, but merely sad.

Of course, Mother took Margot's side; they

always take each other's side. I'm so used to it that I've become completely indifferent to Mother's rebukes and Margot's moodiness. I love them, but only because they're Mother and Margot. I don't give a dash about them as people. As far as I'm concerned, they can go jump in the lake. It's different with Father. When I see him being partial to Margot, approving Margot's every action, praising her, hugging her, I feel a gnawing ache inside, because I'm mad about him. I model myself on Father, and there's no one in the world I love more.

I cling to Father because my contempt of Mother is growing daily and it's only through him that I'm able to retain the last ounce of family feeling I have left. He doesn't understand that I sometimes need to vent my feelings for Mother. He doesn't want to talk about it, and he avoids any discussion involving Mother's failings.

And yet Mother, with all her shortcomings, is tougher for me to deal with. I don't know how I should behave. I can't very well confront her with her carelessness, her sarcasm and her hard-heartedness, yet I can't continue to take the blame for everything.

I tell myself time and again to overlook Mother's bad example. I only want to see her good points, and to look inside myself for what's lacking in her. But it doesn't work, and the worst part is that Father and Mother don't realize their own inadequacies and how much I blame them for letting me down. Are there any parents who can make their children completely happy?

Don't condemn me, but think of me as a person who sometimes reaches bursting point!

Yours, Anne

MONDAY EVENING, 8 NOVEMBER 1943

Dearest Kitty,

If you were to read all my letters in one sitting, you'd be struck by the fact that they were written in a variety of moods. It annoys me to be so dependent on the moods here in the Annexe, but I'm not the only one: we're all subject to them. If I'm engrossed in a book, I have to rearrange my thoughts before I can mingle with other people, because otherwise they might think I was strange. As you can see, I'm currently in the middle of a depression. I couldn't really tell you what set it off, but I think it stems from my cowardice, which confronts me at every turn. This evening, when Bep was still here, the doorbell rang long and loud. I instantly turned white, my stomach churned, and my heart beat wildly – and all because I was afraid.

At night in bed I see myself alone in a dungeon, without Father and Mother. Or I'm roaming the streets, or the Annexe is on fire, or they come in the middle of the night to take us away and I crawl under my bed in desperation. I see everything as if it were actually taking place. And to think it might all happen soon!

Miep often says she envies us because we have such peace and quiet here. That may be true, but she's obviously not thinking about our fear.

I simply can't imagine the world will ever be normal again for us. I do talk about 'after the war', but it's as if I were talking about a castle in the air, something that can never come true.

I see the eight of us in the Annexe as if we were a patch of blue sky surrounded by menacing black clouds. The perfectly round spot on which we're standing is still safe, but the clouds are moving in on us, and the ring between us and the approaching danger is being pulled tighter and tighter. We're surrounded by darkness and danger, and in our desperate search for a way out we keep bumping into each other. We look at the fighting down below and the peace and beauty up above. In the meantime, we've been cut off by the dark mass of clouds, so that we can go neither up nor down. It looms before us like an impenetrable wall, trying to crush us, but not yet able to. I can only cry out and implore, 'Oh, ring, ring, open wide and let us out!'

Yours, Anne

THURSDAY, 11 NOVEMBER 1943

Dearest Kitty,

I have a good title for this chapter:

Ode to My Fountain Pen
In Memoriam

My fountain pen was always one of my most prized possessions; I valued it highly, especially because it had a thick nib, and I can only write neatly with thick nibs. It has led a long and interesting fountain-pen life, which I will summarize below.

When I was nine, my fountain pen (packed in cotton wool) arrived as a 'sample of no commercial value' all the way from Aachen, where my grandmother (the kindly donor) used to live. I lay in bed with flu, while the February winds howled around our flat. This splendid fountain pen came in a red leather case, and I showed it to my girlfriends the first chance I got. Me, Anne Frank, the proud owner of a fountain pen.

When I was ten, I was allowed to take the pen to school, and to my surprise, the teacher even let me write with it. When I was eleven, however, my treasure had to be tucked away again, because my sixth-form teacher allowed us to use only school pens and ink pots. When I was twelve, I started at the Jewish Lyceum and my fountain pen was given a new case in honour of the occasion. Not only did it have room for a pencil, it also had a zip, which was much more impressive. When I was thirteen, the fountain pen went with me to the Annexe, and together we've raced through countless diaries and compositions. I'd turned fourteen and my fountain pen was enjoying the last year of its life with me when . . .

It was just after five on Friday afternoon. I came out of my room and was about to sit down at the table to write when I was roughly pushed to one side to make room for Margot and Father, who wanted to practise their Latin. The fountain pen remained unused on the table, while its owner, sighing, was forced to make do with a very tiny corner of the table, where she began rubbing beans. That's how we remove mould from the beans and restore them to their original state. At a quarter to six I swept the floor, dumped the dirt into a newspaper, along with the rotten beans, and tossed it into the stove. A giant flame shot up, and I thought it was wonderful that the stove, which had been gasping its last breath, had made such a miraculous recovery.

All was quiet again. The Latin students had left, and I sat down at the table to pick up where I'd left off. But no matter where I looked, my fountain pen was nowhere in sight. I took another look. Margot looked, Mother looked, Father looked, Dussel looked. But it had vanished.

'Maybe it fell in the stove, along with the beans!' Margot suggested.

'No, it couldn't have!' I replied.

But that evening, when my fountain pen still hadn't turned up, we all assumed it had been burned, especially because celluloid is highly inflammable. Our darkest fears were confirmed the next day when Father went to empty the stove and discovered the clip, used to fasten it to a pocket, among the ashes. Not a trace of the gold nib was left. 'It must have melted into stone,' Father conjectured.

I'm left with one consolation, small though it may be: my fountain pen was cremated, just as I would like to be some day.

Yours, Anne

Dearest Kitty,

Last night, just as I was falling asleep, Hanneli suddenly appeared before me.

I saw her there, dressed in rags, her face thin and worn. She looked at me with such sadness and reproach in her enormous eyes that I could read the message in them: 'Oh, Anne, why have you deserted me? Help me, help me, rescue me from this hell!'

And I can't help her. I can only stand by and watch while other people suffer and die. All I can do is pray to God to bring her back to us. I saw Hanneli, and no one else, and I understood why. I misjudged her, wasn't mature enough to understand how difficult it was for her. She was devoted to her friend, and it must have seemed as though I were trying to take her away. The poor thing, she must have felt awful! I know, because I recognize the feeling in myself! I had an occasional flash of understanding, but then got selfishly wrapped up again in my own problems and pleasures.

It was horrible of me to treat her that way, and now she was looking at me, oh so helplessly, with her pale face and beseeching eyes. If only I could help her! Dear God, I have everything I could wish for, while fate has her in its deadly clutches. She was as devout as I am, maybe even more so, and she too wanted to do what was right. But then why have I been chosen to live, while she's probably going to die? What's the difference between us? Why are we now so far apart?

To be honest, I hadn't thought of her for months – no, for at least a year. I hadn't forgotten her entirely, and yet it wasn't until I saw her before me that I thought of all her suffering.

Oh, Hanneli, I hope that if you live to the end of the war and return to us, I'll be able to take you in and make up for the wrong I've done you.

But even if I were ever in a position to help, she wouldn't need it more than she does now. I wonder if she ever thinks of me, and what she's feeling.

Merciful God, comfort her, so that at least she won't be alone. Oh, if only You could tell her I'm thinking of her with compassion and love, it might help her go on.

I've got to stop dwelling on this. It won't get

me anywhere. I keep seeing her enormous eyes, and they haunt me. Does Hanneli really and truly believe in God, or has religion merely been foisted upon her? I don't even know that. I never took the trouble to ask.

Hanneli, Hanneli, if only I could take you away, if only I could share everything I have with you. It's too late. I can't help, or undo the wrong I've done. But I'll never forget her again and I'll always pray for her!

Yours, Anne

Anne did not know that Hanneli Goslar had been deported with only her father and little sister. Her mother had died in childbirth, as well as the baby. The Goslars were taken to Bergen-Belsen concentration camp in Poland, where Hanneli's father died. Hanneli and her sister survived and after the war ended they went to live in Israel.

WEDNESDAY, 22 DECEMBER 1943

Dearest Kitty,

A bad case of flu has prevented me from writing to you until today. Being ill here is dreadful. With every cough, I had to duck under the blanket – once, twice, three times – and try

163

to keep from coughing any more. Most of the time the tickle refused to go away, so I had to drink milk with honey, sugar or cough drops. I get dizzy just thinking about all the cures I've been subjected to: sweating out the fever, steam treatment, wet compresses, dry compresses, hot drinks, swabbing my throat, lying still, heating pad, hot-water bottles, lemonade and, every two hours, the thermometer. Will these remedies really make you better? The worst part was when Mr Dussel decided to play doctor and lay his pomaded head on my bare chest to listen to the sounds. Not only did his hair tickle, but I was embarrassed, even though he went to school thirty years ago and does have some kind of medical degree. Why should he lay his head on my heart? After all, he's not my boyfriend! For that matter, he wouldn't be able to tell a healthy sound from an unhealthy one. He'd have to have his ears cleaned first, since he's becoming alarmingly hard of hearing. But enough about my illness. I'm fit as a fiddle again. I've grown almost half an inch and gained two pounds. I'm pale, but itching to get back to my books.

*Ausnahmsweise** (the only word that will do here), we're all getting on well together. No squabbles, though that probably won't last long. There hasn't been such peace and quiet in this house for at least six months.

Bep is still in isolation, but any day now her sister† will no longer be contagious.

For Christmas, we're getting extra cooking oil, sweets and treacle. For Hanukkah, Mr Dussel gave Mrs van Daan and Mother a beautiful cake, which he'd asked Miep to bake. On top of all the work she has to do! Margot and I received a brooch made out of a penny, all bright and shiny. I can't really describe it, but it's lovely.

I also have a Christmas present for Miep and Bep. For a whole month I've saved up the sugar I put on my porridge, and Mr Kleiman has used it to have fondant made.

The weather is drizzly and overcast, the stove stinks, and the food lies heavily on our stomachs, producing a variety of rumbles.

The war is at an impasse, spirits are low.

Yours, Anne

---

* By way of exception
† Bep's sister was suffering from diptheria

Dear Kitty,

As I've written many times before, moods have a tendency to affect us quite a bit here, and in my case it's been getting worse lately. *'Himmelhoch jauchzend, zu Tode betrübt'** certainly applies to me. I'm 'on top of the world' when I think of how fortunate we are and compare myself to other Jewish children, and 'in the depths of despair' when, for example, Mrs Kleiman comes by and talks about Jopie's hockey club, canoe trips, school plays and afternoon teas with friends.

I don't think I'm jealous of Jopie, but I long to have a really good time for once and to laugh so hard it hurts. We're stuck in this house like lepers, especially during winter and the Christmas and New Year holidays. Actually, I shouldn't even be writing this, since it makes me seem so ungrateful, but I can't keep everything to myself, so I'll repeat what I said at the beginning: 'Paper is more patient than people.'

Whenever someone comes in from outside,

---

*A famous line from Goethe: 'On top of the world, or in the depths of despair' with the wind in their clothes and the cold on their cheeks, I feel like burying my head under the blankets to keep from thinking, 'When will we be allowed to breathe fresh air again?' I can't do that – on the contrary, I have to hold my head up high and put a bold face on things, but the thoughts keep coming anyway. Not just once, but over and over.

Believe me, if you've been shut up for a year and a half, it can get to be too much for you sometimes. But feelings can't be ignored, no matter how unjust or ungrateful they seem. I long to ride a bike, dance, whistle, look at the world, feel young and know that I'm free, and yet I can't let it show. Just imagine what would happen if all eight of us were to feel sorry for ourselves or walk around with the discontent clearly visible on our faces. Where would that get us? I sometimes wonder if anyone will ever understand what I mean, if anyone will ever overlook my ingratitude and not worry about whether or not I'm Jewish and merely see me as a teenager badly in need of some good plain fun. I don't know, and I wouldn't be able to talk about it with anyone, since I'm sure I'd start to cry. Crying can bring relief, as long as you don't cry alone. Despite all my theories and efforts, I miss – every day and every hour of the day – having a mother who understands me. That's why with everything I do and write, I imagine the kind of mum I'd like to be to my children later on. The kind of mum who doesn't take everything people say too seriously, but who does take *me* seriously. I find it difficult to describe what I mean, but the word 'mum' says it all. Do you know what I've come up with? In order to give me the feeling of calling my mother something that sounds like 'Mum', I often call her 'Mumsie'. Sometimes I shorten it to 'Mums': an imperfect 'Mum'. I wish I could honour her by removing the 's'. It's a good thing she doesn't realize this, since it would only make her unhappy.

Well, that's enough of that. My writing has raised me somewhat from 'the depths of despair'.

Yours, Anne

SUNDAY, 2 JANUARY 1944

Dearest Kitty,

This morning, when I had nothing to do, I leafed through the pages of my diary and came across so many letters dealing with the subject of 'Mother' in such strong terms that I was shocked. I said to myself, 'Anne, is that really you talking about hate? Oh, Anne, how could you?'

I continued to sit with the open book in my hand and wonder why I was filled with so much anger and hate that I had to confide it all to you. I tried to understand the Anne of last year and make apologies for her, because as long as I leave you with these accusations and don't attempt to explain what prompted them, my conscience won't be clear. I was suffering then (and still do) from moods that kept my head underwater (figuratively speaking) and allowed me to see things only from my own perspective, without calmly considering what the others – those whom I, with my mercurial temperament, had hurt or offended – had said, and then behaving as they would have done.

I hid inside myself, thought of no one but myself and calmly wrote down all my joy, sarcasm and sorrow in my diary. Because this diary has become a kind of scrapbook, it means a great deal to me, but I could easily write 'over and done with' on many of its pages.

I was furious at Mother (and still am a lot of the time). It's true, she didn't understand me, but I didn't understand her either. Because she loved me, she was tender and affectionate, but because of the difficult situations I put her in, and the sad circumstances in which she found herself, she was nervous and irritable, so I can understand why she was often short with me.

I was offended, took it far too much to heart and was insolent and beastly to her, which, in turn, made her unhappy. We were caught in a vicious circle of unpleasantness and sorrow. Not a very happy period for either of us, but at least it's coming to an end. I didn't want to see what was going on, and I felt very sorry for myself, but that's understandable too.

Those violent outbursts on paper are simply expressions of anger that, in normal life, I could have worked off by locking myself in my room and stamping my foot a few times or calling Mother names behind her back.

The period of tearfully passing judgement on Mother is over. I've grown wiser and Mother's nerves are a bit steadier. Most of the time I manage to hold my tongue when I'm annoyed, and she does too; so on the surface, we seem to be getting along better. But there's one thing I can't do, and that's to love Mother with the devotion of a child.

I soothe my conscience with the thought that it's better for unkind words to be down on paper than for Mother to have to carry them around in her heart.

Yours, Anne

THURSDAY, 6 JANUARY 1944

Dearest Kitty,

Today I have two things to confess. It's going to take a long time, but I have to tell them to someone, and you're the most likely candidate, since I know you'll keep a secret, no matter what happens.

The first is about Mother. As you know, I've frequently complained about her and then tried my best to be nice. I've suddenly realized what's wrong with her. Mother has said that she sees us more as friends than as daughters. That's all very nice, of course, except that a friend can't take the place of a mother. I need my mother to set a good example and be a person I can respect, but in most matters she's an example of what *not* to do. I have the feeling that Margot thinks so differently about these things that she'd never be able to understand what I've just told you. And Father avoids all conversations having to do with Mother.

I imagine a mother as a woman who, first and foremost, possesses a great deal of tact, especially towards her adolescent children, and not one who, like Mumsie, pokes fun at me when I cry. Not because I'm in pain, but because of other things.

This may seem trivial, but there's one incident I've never forgiven her for. It happened one day when I had to go to the dentist. Mother and Margot planned to go with me and agreed I should take my bicycle. When the dentist was finished and we were back outside, Margot and Mother very sweetly informed me that they were going into town to buy or look at something, I don't remember what, and of course I wanted to go along. But they said I couldn't come because I had my bike with me. Tears of rage rushed to my eyes, and Margot and Mother began laughing at me. I was so furious that I stuck my tongue out at them, right there on the street. A little old lady happened to be passing by, and she looked terribly shocked. I cycled home and must have cried for hours. Strangely enough, even though Mother has wounded me thousands of times, this particular wound still stings whenever I think of how angry I was.

I find it difficult to confess the second one because it's about myself. I'm not prudish, Kitty, and yet every time they give a blow-by-blow account of their trips to the lavatory, which they often do, my whole body rises in revolt.

Yesterday I read an article on blushing by Sis Heyster. It was as if she'd addressed it directly to me. Not that I blush easily, but the rest of the article did apply. What she basically says is that during puberty girls withdraw into themselves and begin thinking about the wondrous changes taking place in their bodies. I feel that too, which probably accounts for my recent embarrassment over Margot, Mother and Father. On the other hand, Margot is a lot shyer than I am, and yet she's not in the least embarrassed.

Dearest Kitty,

My longing for someone to talk to has become so unbearable that I somehow took it into my head to select Peter for this role. On the few occasions when I have gone to Peter's room during the day, I've always thought it was nice and cosy. But Peter's too polite to show someone the door when they're bothering him, so I've never dared to stay long. I've always been afraid he'd think I was a pest. I've been looking for an excuse to linger in his room and get him talking without his noticing, and yesterday I got my chance. Peter, you see, is currently going through a crossword-puzzle craze, and he doesn't do anything else all day. I was helping him, and we soon ended up sitting across from each other at his table, Peter on the chair and me on the divan.

It gave me a wonderful feeling when I looked into his dark blue eyes and saw how bashful my unexpected visit had made him. I could read his innermost thoughts, and in his face I saw a look of helplessness and uncertainty as to how to behave, and at the same time a flicker of awareness of his masculinity. I saw his shyness, and I melted. I wanted to say, 'Tell me about yourself. Look beneath my chatty exterior.' But I found that it was easier to think up questions than to ask them.

The evening came to a close, and nothing happened, except that I told him about the article on blushing. Not what I wrote you, of course, just that he would grow more secure as he got older.

That night I lay in bed and cried my eyes out, all the while making sure no one could hear me. The idea that I had to beg Peter for favours was simply revolting. But people will do almost anything to satisfy their longings; take me, for example, I've made up my mind to visit Peter more often and, somehow, get him to talk to me.

You mustn't think I'm in love with Peter, because I'm not. If the van Daans had had a daughter instead of a son, I'd have tried to make friends with her.

This morning I woke up just before seven and immediately remembered what I'd been dreaming about. I was sitting on a chair and across from me was Peter ... Peter Schiff. We were looking at Mary Bos's sketchbook. The dream was so vivid I can even remember some of the drawings. But that wasn't all – the dream went on. Peter's eyes suddenly met mine, and I stared for a long time into those velvety brown eyes. Then he said very softly, 'If I'd only known, I'd have come to you long ago!' I turned abruptly away, overcome by emotion. And then I felt a soft, oh-so-cool and gentle cheek against mine, and it felt so good, so good . . .

At that point I woke up, still feeling his cheek against mine and his brown eyes staring deep into my heart, so deep that he could read how much I'd loved him and how much I still do. Again my eyes filled with tears, and I was sad because I'd lost him once more, and yet at the same time glad because I knew with certainty that Peter is still the only one for me.

It's funny, but I often have such vivid images in my dreams. One night I saw Grammy so clearly that I could even make out her skin of soft, crinkly velvet. Another time Grandma appeared to me as a guardian angel. After that it was Hanneli, who still symbolizes to me the suffering of my friends as well as that of Jews in general, so that when I'm praying for her, I'm also praying for all the Jews and all those in need.

And now Peter, my dearest Peter. I've never had such a clear mental image of him. I don't need a photograph, I can see him oh so well.

Yours, Anne

WEDNESDAY, 12 JANUARY 1944

Dearest Kitty,

Bep's been back for the last two weeks, though her sister won't be allowed back at school until next week. Bep herself spent two days in bed with a bad cold. Miep and Jan were also out for two days, with upset stomachs.

I'm currently going through a dance and ballet craze and am diligently practising my dance steps every evening. I've made an ultramodern dance costume out of a lacy lavender petticoat belonging to Mumsie. Tape is threaded through the top and tied just above the bust. A pink corded ribbon completes the ensemble. I tried to turn my gym shoes into ballet slippers, but with no success. My stiff limbs are well on the way to becoming as supple as they used to be. A terrific exercise is to sit on the floor, place a heel in each hand and raise both legs in the air. I have to sit on a cushion, because otherwise my poor backside really takes a beating.

Everyone here is reading a book called *Salute to Freedom*. Mother thought it was extremely good because it describes a number of adolescent problems. I thought to myself, a bit ironically, 'Why don't you take more interest in your own adolescents first!'

I think Mother believes that Margot and I have a better relationship with our parents than anyone in the whole wide world, and that no mother is more involved in the lives of her children than she is. She must have my sister in mind, since I don't believe Margot has the same problems and thoughts as I do. Far be it from me to point out to Mother that one of her daughters is not at all what she imagines. She'd be completely bewildered, and anyway, she'd never be able to change; I'd like to spare her that grief, especially since I know that everything would remain the same. Mother does sense that Margot loves her much more than I do, but she thinks I'm just going through a phase.

Margot's much nicer. She seems a lot different from what she used to be. She's not nearly as catty these days and is becoming a real friend. She no longer thinks of me as a little baby who doesn't count.

It's funny, but I can sometimes see myself as others see me. I take a leisurely look at the person called 'Anne Frank' and browse through the pages of her life as though she were a stranger.

Everything has become much worse here. But you already knew that. Now God has sent someone to help me: Peter. I fondle my pendant, press it to my lips and think, 'What do I care! Petel is mine and nobody knows it!' With this in mind, I can rise above every nasty remark. Which of the people here would suspect that so much is going on in the mind of a teenage girl?

SATURDAY, 22 JANUARY 1944

Dearest Kitty,

Can you tell me why people go to such lengths to hide their real selves? Or why I always behave very differently when I'm in the company of others? Why do people have so little trust in one another? I know there must be a reason, but sometimes I think it's horrible that you can't ever confide in anyone, not even those closest to you.

It seems as if I've grown up since the night I had that dream, as if I've become more independent. You'll be amazed when I tell you that even my attitude towards the van Daans has changed. I've stopped looking at all the discussions and arguments from my family's biased point of view. What's brought on such a radical change? Well, you see, I suddenly realized that if Mother had been different, if she'd been a real mum, our relationship would have been very, very different. Mrs van Daan is by no means a wonderful person, yet half the arguments could have been avoided if Mother hadn't been so hard to deal with every time they got on to a tricky subject. Mrs van Daan does have one good point, though: you can talk to her. She may be selfish, stingy and underhanded, but she'll readily back down as long as you don't provoke her and make her unreasonable. This tactic doesn't work every time, but if you're patient, you can keep trying and see how far you get.

All the conflicts about our upbringing, about not pampering children, about the food – about everything, absolutely everything – might have taken a different turn if we'd remained open and on friendly terms instead of always seeing the worst side.

I know exactly what you're going to say, Kitty. 'But, Anne, are these words really coming from your lips? From you, who have had to put up with so many unkind words from upstairs? From you, who are aware of all the injustices?'

And yet they are coming from me. I want to take a fresh look at things and form my own opinion, not just ape my parents, as in the proverb 'The apple never falls far from the tree'. I want to re-examine the van Daans and decide for myself what's true and what's been blown out of proportion. If I end up being disappointed in them, I can always side with Father and Mother. But if not, I can try to change their attitude. And if that doesn't work, I'll have to stick with my own opinions and judgement. I'll take every opportunity to speak openly to Mrs van D. about our many differences and not be afraid – despite my reputation as a smart alec – to offer my impartial opinion. I won't say anything negative about my own family, though that doesn't mean I won't defend them if somebody else does, and as of today, my gossiping is a thing of the past.

Up till now I was absolutely convinced that the van Daans were entirely to blame for the quarrels, but now I'm sure the fault was largely ours. We were right as far as the issues were concerned, but intelligent people (such as ourselves!) should have more insight into how to deal with others.

I hope I've got at least a touch of that insight, and that I'll find an occasion to put it to good use.

Yours, Anne

FRIDAY, 28 JANUARY 1944

Dearest Kitty,

In recent weeks I've developed a great liking for family trees and the genealogical tables of royal families. I've come to the conclusion that once you begin your search, you have to keep digging deeper and deeper into the past, which leads you to even more interesting discoveries.

Although I'm extremely diligent when it comes to my schoolwork and can pretty much follow the BBC Home Service on the radio, I still spend many of my Sundays sorting out and looking over my film-star collection, which has grown to a very respectable size. Mr Kugler makes me happy every Monday by bringing me a copy of *Cinema & Theatre* magazine. The less worldly members of our household often refer to this small indulgence as a waste of money, yet they never fail to be surprised at how accurately I can list the actors in any given film, even after a year. Bep, who often goes to the cinema with her boyfriend on her day off, tells me on Saturday the name of the film they're going to see, and I then proceed to rattle off the names of the leading actors and actresses and the reviews. Mums recently remarked that I wouldn't need to go to the cinema later on, because I know all the plots, the names of the stars and the reviews by heart.

Whenever I come sailing in with a new hair-style, I can read the disapproval on their faces, and I can be sure someone will ask which film star I'm trying to imitate. My reply, that it's my own invention, is greeted with scepticism. As for the hair-do, it doesn't hold its set for more than half an hour. By that time I'm so sick and tired of their remarks that I race to the bathroom and restore my hair to its normal mass of curls.

Yours, Anne

FRIDAY, 28 JANUARY 1944

Dearest Kitty,

This morning I was wondering whether you ever felt like a cow, having to chew my stale news over and over again until you're so fed up with the monotonous fare that you yawn and secretly wish Anne would dig up something new.

Sorry, I know you find it dull as ditchwater, but imagine how sick and tired I am of hearing the same old stuff. If the talk at mealtimes isn't about politics or good food, then Mother or Mrs van D. trot out stories about their childhood that we've heard a thousand times before, or Dussel goes on and on about beautiful race-horses, his Charlotte's extensive wardrobe, leaky rowing boats, boys who can swim at the age of four, aching muscles and frightened patients. It all boils down to this: whenever one of the eight of us opens his mouth, the other seven can finish the story for him. We know the punchline of every joke before it gets told, so that whoever's telling it is left to laugh alone. The various milkmen, grocers and butchers of the two former housewives have been praised to the skies or run into the ground so many times that in our imaginations they've grown as old as Methuselah; there's absolutely no chance of anything new or fresh being brought up for discussion in the Annexe.

Still, all this might be bearable if only the grown-ups weren't in the habit of repeating the stories we hear from Mr Kleiman, Jan or Miep, each time embellishing them with a few details of their own, so that I often have to pinch my arm under the table to keep myself from setting the enthusiastic storyteller on the right track. Little children, such as Anne, must never, ever correct their elders, no matter how many blunders they make or how often they let their imaginations run away with them.

Jan and Mr Kleiman love talking about

people who have gone underground or into hiding; they know we're eager to hear about others in our situation and that we truly sympathize with the sorrow of those who've been arrested as well as the joy of prisoners who've been freed.

Going underground or into hiding has become as routine as the proverbial pipe and slippers that used to await the man of the house after a long day at work. There are many resistance groups, such as Free Netherlands, that forge identity cards, provide financial support to those in hiding, organize hiding places and find work for young Christians who go underground. It's amazing how much these generous and unselfish people do, risking their own lives to help and save others.

The best example of this is our own helpers, who have managed to pull us through so far and will hopefully bring us safely to shore, because otherwise they'll find themselves sharing the fate of those they're trying to protect. Never have they uttered a single word about the burden we must be, never have they complained that we're too much trouble. They come upstairs every day and talk to the men about business and politics, to the women about food and wartime difficulties and to the children about books and newspapers. They put on their most cheerful expressions, bring flowers and gifts for birthdays and special occasions and are always ready to do what they can. That's something we should never forget; while others display their heroism in battle or against the Germans, our helpers prove theirs every day by their good spirits and affection.

Yours, Anne

SUNDAY, 30 JANUARY 1944

My dearest Kit,

Another Sunday has rolled around; I don't mind them as much as I did in the beginning, but they're boring enough.

I still haven't gone to the warehouse yet, but maybe sometime soon. Last night I went downstairs in the dark, all by myself, after having been there with Father a few nights before. I stood at the top of the stairs while German planes flew back and forth, and I knew I was on my own, that I couldn't count on others for support. My fear vanished. I looked up at the sky and trusted in God.

I have an intense need to be alone. Father has noticed I'm not my usual self, but I can't tell him what's bothering me. All I want to do is scream, 'Let me be, leave me alone!'

Who knows, perhaps the day will come when I'm left alone more than I'd like!

Anne Frank

THURSDAY, 3 FEBRUARY 1944

Dearest Kitty,

Invasion fever is mounting daily throughout the country. If you were here, I'm sure you'd be as impressed as I am at the many preparations, though you'd no doubt laugh at all the fuss we're making. Who knows, it may all be for nothing!

The papers are full of invasion news and are driving everyone insane with such statements as: 'In the event of a British landing in Holland, the Germans will do what they can to defend the country, even flooding it, if necessary.' They've published maps of Holland with the potential flood areas marked. Since large portions of Amsterdam were shaded in, our first question was what we should do if the water in the streets rose to above our waists. This tricky question elicited a variety of responses:

'It'll be impossible to walk or ride a bike, so we'll have to wade through the water.'

'Don't be silly. We'll have to try and swim. We'll all put on our bathing suits and caps and swim underwater as much as we can, so nobody can see we're Jews.'

'Rubbish! I can just imagine the ladies swimming with the rats biting their legs!' (That was a man, of course; we'll see who screams loudest!)

'We won't even be able to leave the house. The warehouse is so unstable it'll collapse if there's a flood.'

'Listen, everyone, all joking aside, we really ought to try and get a boat.'

'Why bother? I have a better idea. We can each take a packing case from the attic and row with a wooden spoon.'

'I'm going to walk on stilts. I used to be a wizard at it when I was young.'

'Jan Gies won't need to. He'll let his wife ride piggyback, and then Miep will be on stilts.'

So now you have a rough idea of what's going on, don't you, Kit? This light-hearted banter is all very amusing, but reality will prove otherwise. The second question about the invasion was bound to arise: what should we do if the Germans evacuate Amsterdam?

'Leave the city along with the others. Disguise ourselves as well as we can.'

'Whatever happens, don't go outside! The best thing to do is to stay put! The Germans are capable of herding the entire population of Holland into Germany, where they'll all die.'

'Of course we'll stay here. This is the safest place. We'll try to talk Kleiman and his family into coming here to live with us. We'll somehow get hold of a bag of wood shavings, so we can sleep on the floor. Let's ask Miep and Kleiman to bring some blankets, just in case. And we'll order some extra grain to supplement the sixty-five pounds we already have. Jan can try to find some more beans. At the moment we've got about sixty-five pounds of beans and ten pounds of split peas. And don't forget the fifty tins of vegetables.'

'What about the rest, Mother? Give us the latest figures.'

'Ten tins of fish, forty tins of milk, twenty pounds of powdered milk, three bottles of oil, four pots of butter, four jars of meat, two big jars of strawberries, two jars of raspberries, twenty jars of tomatoes, ten pounds of oatmeal, nine pounds of rice. That's it.'

Our supplies are holding out fairly well. All the same, we have to feed the office staff, which means dipping into our reserves every week, so it's not as much as it seems. We have enough coal and firewood, candles too.

'Let's all make little moneybags to hide in our clothes so we can take our money with us if we need to leave here.'

'We can make lists of what to take first in case we have to run for it, and pack our rucksacks in advance.'

'When the time comes, we'll put two people on lookout, one in the loft at the front of the house and one at the back.'

'Hang on, what's the use of so much food if there isn't any water, gas or electricity?'

'We'll have to cook on the stove. Filter the

water and boil it. We should clean some big jugs and fill them with water. We can also store water in the three pans we use for preserving, and in the tin bath.'

'Besides, we still have about two hundred and thirty pounds of winter potatoes in the spice storeroom.'

All day long that's all I hear. Invasion, invasion, nothing but invasion. Arguments about going hungry, dying, bombs, fire extinguishers, sleeping bags, identity cards, poison gas, etc., etc. Not exactly cheerful.

A good example of the explicit warnings of the male contingent is the following conversation with Jan:

Annexe: 'We're afraid that when the Germans retreat, they'll take the entire population with them.'

Jan: 'That's impossible. They haven't got enough trains.'

Annexe: 'Trains? Do you really think they'd put civilians on trains? Absolutely not. Everyone would have to hoof it.' (Or, as Dussel always says, *per pedes apostolorum**.)

---

* By the feet of the Apostles

Jan: 'I can't believe that. You're always looking on the dark side. What reason would they have to round up all the civilians and take them along?'

Annexe: 'Don't you remember Goebbels saying that if the Germans have to go, they'll slam the doors to all the occupied territories behind them?'

Jan: 'They've said a lot of things.'

Annexe: 'Do you think the Germans are too noble or humane to do it? Their reasoning is: if we go under, we'll drag everyone else down with us.'

Jan: 'You can say what you like, I just don't believe it.'

Annexe: 'It's always the same old story. No one wants to see the danger until it's staring them in the face.'

Jan: 'But you don't know anything for sure. You're just making an assumption.'

Annexe: 'Because we've already been through it all ourselves. First in Germany and then here. What do you think's happening in Russia?'

Jan: 'You shouldn't include the Jews. I don't think anyone knows what's going on in Russia.

The British and the Russians are probably exaggerating for propaganda purposes, just like the Germans.'

Annexe: 'Absolutely not. The BBC has always told the truth. And even if the news is slightly exaggerated, the facts are bad enough as they are. You can't deny that millions of peace-loving citizens in Poland and Russia have been murdered or gassed.'

I'll spare you the rest of our conversations. I'm very calm and take no notice of all the fuss. I've reached the point where I hardly care whether I live or die. The world will keep on turning without me, and I can't do anything to change events anyway. I'll just let matters take their course and concentrate on studying and hope that everything will be all right in the end.

Yours, Anne

SATURDAY, 12 FEBRUARY 1944

Dearest Kitty,

The sun is shining, the sky is deep blue, there's a magnificent breeze, and I'm longing –

really longing – for everything: conversation, freedom, friends, being alone. I long . . . to cry! I feel as if I were about to explode. I know crying would help, but I can't cry. I'm restless. I walk from one room to another, breathe through the crack in the window frame, feel my heart beating as if to say, 'Fulfil my longing at last . . .'

I think spring is inside me. I feel spring awakening, I feel it in my entire body and soul. I have to force myself to act normally. I'm in a state of utter confusion, don't know what to read, what to write, what to do. I only know that I'm longing for something . . .

Yours, Anne

WEDNESDAY, 16 FEBRUARY 1944

Peter and I hadn't talked to each other all day, except for a few meaningless words. It was too cold to go up to the attic, and anyway, it was Margot's birthday. At twelve thirty he came to look at the presents and hung around chatting longer than was strictly necessary, something he'd never have done otherwise. But I got my chance in the afternoon. Since I felt like spoiling Margot on her birthday, I went to get the coffee, and after that the potatoes. When I came to Peter's room, he immediately took his papers off the stairs, and I asked if I should close the trapdoor to the attic.

'Yes,' he said, 'go ahead. When you're ready to come back down, just knock and I'll open it for you.'

I thanked him, went upstairs and spent at least ten minutes searching around in the barrel for the smallest potatoes. My back started aching, and the attic was cold. Naturally, I didn't bother to knock but opened the trapdoor myself. But he obligingly got up and took the pan out of my hands.

'I did my best, but I couldn't find any smaller ones.'

'Did you look in the big barrel?'

'Yes, I've been through them all.'

By this time I was at the bottom of the stairs, and he examined the pan of potatoes he was still holding. 'Oh, but these are fine,' he said, and added, as I took the pan from him, 'My compliments!'

As he said this, he gave me such a warm, tender look that I started glowing inside. I could tell he wanted to please me, but since he couldn't make a long complimentary speech, he said everything with his eyes. I understood him so well and was very grateful. It still makes me happy to think back to those words and that look!

When I went downstairs, Mother said she needed more potatoes, this time for dinner, so I volunteered to go back up. When I entered Peter's room, I apologized for disturbing him again. As I was going up the stairs, he stood up, went over to stand between the stairs and the wall, grabbed my arm and tried to stop me.

'I'll go,' he said. 'I have to go upstairs anyway.'

I replied that it wasn't really necessary, that I didn't have to get only the small ones this time. Convinced, he let go of my arm. On my way back, he opened the trapdoor and once again took the pan from me. Standing by the door, I asked, 'What are you working on?'

'French,' he replied.

I asked if I could take a look at his lessons. Then I went to wash my hands and sat down across from him on the divan.

After I'd explained some French to him, we began to talk. He told me that after the war he wanted to go to the Dutch East Indies and live on a rubber plantation. He talked about his life at home, the black market and what a hopeless case he is. I told him he had a big inferiority complex. He talked about the war, saying that Russia and England were bound to go to war against each other, and about the Jews. He said life would have been much easier if he'd been a Christian or could become one after the war. I asked if he wanted to be baptized, but that wasn't what he meant either. He said he'd never be able to feel like a Christian, but that after the war he'd make sure nobody would know he was Jewish. I felt a momentary pang. It's such a shame he still has a touch of dishonesty in him.

Peter added, 'The Jews have been and always will be the chosen people!'

I answered, 'Just this once, I hope they'll be chosen for something good!'

But we went on chatting very pleasantly, about Father, about judging human character and all sorts of things, so many that I can't even remember them all.

I left at a quarter past five, because Bep had arrived.

That evening he said something else I thought was nice. We were talking about the picture of a film star I'd once given him, which has been hanging in his room for at least a year and a half. He liked it so much that I offered to give him a few more.

'No,' he replied, 'I'd rather keep the one I've got. I look at it every day, and the people in it have become my friends.'

I now have a better understanding of why he always hugs Mouschi so tightly. He obviously needs affection too. I forgot to mention something else he was talking about. He said, 'No, I'm not afraid, except when it comes to things about myself, but I'm working on that.'

Peter has a huge inferiority complex. For example, he always thinks he's so stupid and we're so clever. When I help him with French, he thanks me a thousand times. One of these days I'm going to say, 'Oh, cut it out! You're much better at English and geography!'

Anne Frank

What happens in other people's houses during the rest of the week happens here in the Annexe on Sundays. While other people put on their best clothes and go strolling in the sun, we scrub, sweep and do the washing.

Eight o'clock. Though the rest of us prefer to lie in, Dussel gets up at eight. He goes to the bathroom, then downstairs, then up again and then to the bathroom, where he devotes a whole hour to washing himself.

Nine thirty. The stoves are lit, the blackout screen is taken down, and Mr van Daan heads for the bathroom. One of my Sunday morning ordeals is having to lie in bed and look at Dussel's back when he's praying. I know it sounds strange, but a praying Dussel is a terrible sight to behold. It's not that he cries or gets sentimental, not at all, but he does spend a quarter of an hour – an entire fifteen minutes – rocking from his toes to his heels. Back and forth, back and forth. It goes on for ever, and if I don't shut my eyes tight, my head starts to spin.

Ten fifteen. The van Daans whistle; the bathroom's free. In the Frank family quarters, the first sleepy faces are beginning to emerge from their pillows. Then everything happens fast, fast, fast. Margot and I take turns doing the washing. Since it's quite cold downstairs, we put on trousers and headscarves. Meanwhile, Father is busy in the bathroom. Either Margot or I have a turn in the bathroom at eleven, and then we're all clean.

Eleven thirty. Breakfast. I won't dwell on this, since there's enough talk about food without my bringing the subject up as well.

Twelve fifteen. We each go our separate ways. Father, clad in overalls, gets down on his hands and knees and brushes the rug so vigorously that the room is enveloped in a cloud of dust. Mr Dussel makes the beds (all wrong, of course), always whistling the same Beethoven violin concerto as he goes about his work. Mother can be heard shuffling around the attic as she hangs up the washing. Mr van Daan puts on his hat and disappears into the lower regions, usually followed by Peter and Mouschi. Mrs van D. dons a long apron, a black woollen jacket and overshoes, winds a red woollen scarf around her head, scoops up a bundle of dirty laundry and, with a well-rehearsed washerwoman's nod, heads downstairs. Margot and I do the dishes and tidy up the room.

My dearest Kitty,

The weather's been wonderful since yesterday, and I've perked up quite a bit. My writing, the best thing I have, is coming along well. I go to the attic almost every morning to get the stale air out of my lungs. This morning when I went there, Peter was busy cleaning up. He finished quickly and came over to where I was sitting on my favourite spot on the floor. The two of us looked out at the blue sky, the bare chestnut tree glistening with dew, the seagulls and other birds glinting with silver as they swooped through the air, and we were so moved and entranced that we couldn't speak. He stood with his head against a thick beam, while I sat. We breathed in the air, looked outside and both felt that the spell shouldn't be broken with words. We remained like this for a long while, and by the time he had to go to the loft to chop wood, I knew he was a good, decent boy. He climbed the ladder to the loft, and I followed; during the fifteen minutes he was chopping wood, we didn't say a word either. I watched him from where I was standing, and could see he was obviously doing his best to chop the right way and show off his strength. But I also looked out of the open window, letting my eyes roam over a large part of Amsterdam, over the rooftops and on to the horizon, a strip of blue so pale it was almost invisible.

'As long as this exists,' I thought, 'this sunshine and this cloudless sky, and as long as I can enjoy it, how can I be sad?'

The best remedy for those who are frightened, lonely or unhappy is to go outside, somewhere they can be alone, alone with the sky, nature and God. For then and only then can you feel that everything is as it should be and that God wants people to be happy amid nature's beauty and simplicity.

As long as this exists, and that should be for ever, I know that there will be solace for every sorrow, whatever the circumstances. I firmly believe that nature can bring comfort to all who suffer.

Oh, who knows, perhaps it won't be long before I can share this overwhelming feeling of happiness with someone who feels the same as I do.

Yours, Anne

PS. Thoughts: To Peter.

We've been missing out on so much here, so very much, and for such a long time. I miss it just as much as you do. I'm not talking about external things, since we're well provided for in that sense; I mean the internal things. Like you, I long for freedom and fresh air, but I think we've been amply compensated for their loss. On the inside, I mean.

This morning, when I was sitting in front of the window and taking a long, deep look outside at God and nature, I was happy, just plain happy. Peter, as long as people feel that kind of happiness within themselves, the joy of nature, health and much more besides, they'll always be able to recapture that happiness.

Riches, prestige, everything can be lost. But the happiness in your own heart can only be dimmed; it will always be there, as long as you live, to make you happy again.

Whenever you're feeling lonely or sad, try going to the loft on a beautiful day and looking outside. Not at the houses and the rooftops, but at the sky. As long as you can look fearlessly at the sky, you'll know that you're pure within and will find happiness once more.

SUNDAY, 27 FEBRUARY 1944

My dearest Kitty,

From early in the morning till late at night, all I do is think about Peter. I fall asleep with his image before my eyes, dream about him and wake up with him still looking at me.

I have the strong feeling that Peter and I aren't really as different as we may seem on the surface, and I'll explain why: neither Peter nor I have a mother. His is too superficial, likes to flirt and doesn't concern herself much with what goes on in his head. Mine takes an active interest in my life, but has no tact, sensitivity or motherly understanding.

Both Peter and I are struggling with our innermost feelings. We're still unsure of ourselves and are too vulnerable, emotionally, to be dealt with so roughly. Whenever that happens, I want to run outside or hide my feelings. Instead, I bang the pots and pans, splash the water and am generally noisy, so that everyone wishes I were miles away. Peter's reaction is to shut himself away, say little, sit quietly and daydream, all the while carefully hiding his true self.

But how and when will we finally reach each other?

I don't know how much longer I can continue to keep this yearning under control.

Yours, Anne M. Frank

THURSDAY, 2 MARCH 1944

Dearest Kitty,

Margot and I were in the attic together today. I can't enjoy being there with her the way I imagine it'd be with Peter (or someone else). I know she feels the same about most things as I do!

While washing up, Bep began talking to Mother and Mrs van Daan about how discouraged she gets. What help did those two offer her? Our tactless mother, especially, only made things go from bad to worse. Do you know what her advice was? That she should think about all the other people in the world who are suffering! How can thinking about the misery of others help if you're miserable yourself? I said as much. Their response, of course, was that I should stay out of conversations of this sort.

The grown-ups are such idiots! As if Peter, Margot, Bep and I didn't all have the same feelings. The only thing that helps is a mother's love, or that of a very, very close friend. But these two mothers don't understand the first thing about us! Perhaps Mrs van Daan does, a bit more than Mother. Oh, I wish I could have said something to poor Bep, something that I know from my own experience would have helped. But Father came between us, pushing me roughly aside. They're all so stupid!

I also talked to Margot about Father and Mother, about how nice it could be here if they weren't so aggravating. We'd be able to organize evenings in which everyone could take turns discussing a given subject. But we've already been through all that. It's impossible for me to talk here! Mr van Daan goes on the offensive, Mother gets sarcastic and can't say *anything* in a normal voice, Father doesn't feel like taking part, nor does Mr Dussel, and Mrs van D. is attacked so often that she just sits there with a red face, hardly able to put up a fight any more. And what about us? We aren't allowed to have an opinion! My, my, aren't they progressive! Not have an opinion! People can tell you to shut up, but they can't keep you from having an opinion. You can't forbid someone to have an opinion, no matter how young they are! The only thing that would help Bep, Margot, Peter and me would be great love and devotion, which we don't get here. And no one, especially not the idiotic sages around here, is capable of understanding us, since we're more sensitive and much more advanced in our thinking than any of them ever suspect!

*

At the moment, Mother's grumbling at me again; she's clearly jealous because I talk to Mrs van Daan more than to her. What do I care!

I managed to get hold of Peter this afternoon, and we talked for at least forty-five minutes. He wanted to tell me something about himself, but didn't find it easy. He finally got it out, though it took a long time. I honestly didn't know whether it was better for me to stay or to go. But I wanted so much to help him! I told him about Bep and how tactless our mothers are. He told me that his parents argue constantly, about politics and cigarettes and all kinds of things. As I've told you before, Peter's very shy, but not too shy to admit that he'd be perfectly happy not to see his parents for a year or two. 'My father isn't as nice as he looks,' he said. 'But in the matter of the cigarettes, Mother's absolutely right.'

I also told him about my mother. But he came to Father's defence. He thought he was a 'terrific chap'.

Tonight, when I was hanging up my apron after washing up, he called me over and asked me not to say anything downstairs about his parents' having had another argument and not being on speaking terms. I promised, though I'd already told Margot. But I'm sure Margot won't pass it on.

'Oh no, Peter,' I said, 'you don't have to worry about me. I've learned not to blab everything I hear. I never repeat what you tell me.'

He was glad to hear that. I also told him what terrible gossips we are, and said, 'Margot's quite right, of course, when she says I'm not being honest, because as much as I want to stop gossiping, there's nothing I like better than discussing Mr Dussel.'

'It's good that you admit it,' he said. He blushed, and his sincere compliment almost embarrassed me too.

Then we talked about 'upstairs' and 'downstairs' some more. Peter was really rather surprised to hear that we don't like his parents. 'Peter,' I said, 'you know I'm always honest, so why shouldn't I tell you this as well? We can see their faults too.'

I added, 'Peter, I'd really like to help you. Will you let me? You're caught in an awkward position, and I know, even though you don't say anything, that it upsets you.'

'Oh, your help is always welcome!'

'Maybe it'd be better for you to talk to Father. You can tell him anything, he won't pass it on.'

'I know, he's a real pal.'

'You like him a lot, don't you?'

Peter nodded, and I continued, 'Well, he likes you too, you know!'

He looked up quickly and blushed. It was really touching to see how happy these few words made him. 'You think so?' he asked.

'Yes,' I said. 'You can tell from the little things he lets slip now and then.'

Then Mr van Daan came in to do some dictating. Peter's a 'terrific chap', just like Father!

Yours, Anne M. Frank

FRIDAY, 3 MARCH 1944

My dearest Kitty,

When I looked into the candle tonight, I felt calm and happy again. It seems Grandma is in that candle, and it's Grandma who watches over and protects me and makes me feel happy again. But . . . there's someone else who governs all my moods and that's ... Peter. I went to get the potatoes today, and while I was standing on the stairway with my pan full, he asked, 'What did you do during lunch break?'

I sat down on the stairs, and we began to talk. The potatoes didn't make it to the kitchen until five fifteen (an hour after I'd gone to get them). Peter didn't say anything more about his parents; we just talked about books and about the past. Oh, he gazes at me with such warmth in his eyes; I don't think it will take much for me to fall in love with him.

He brought the subject up this evening. I went to his room after peeling potatoes and remarked on how hot it was. 'You can tell the temperature by looking at Margot and me, because we turn white when it's cold and red when it's hot,' I said.

'In love?' he asked.

'Why should I be in love?' It was a pretty silly answer (or, rather, question).

'Why not?' he said, and then it was time for dinner.

What did he mean? Today I finally managed to ask him whether my chatter bothered him.

All he said was, 'Oh, it's fine with me!' I can't tell how much of his reply was due to shyness.

Kitty, I sound like someone who's in love and can talk about nothing but her dearest darling. And Peter is a darling. Will I ever be able to tell him that? Only if he thinks the same of me, but I'm the kind of person you have to treat with kid gloves, I know that all too well. And he likes to be left alone, so I don't know how much he likes me. In any case, we're getting to know each other a little better. I wish we dared to say more. But who knows, maybe that time will come sooner than I think! Once or twice a day he gives me a knowing glance, I wink back, and we're both happy. It seems insane to talk about his being happy, and yet I have the overwhelming feeling he thinks the same way I do.

Yours, Anne M. Frank

Anne experienced an intense longing for friendship, affection and tenderness. In the Annexe there was only Peter for Anne to turn to. She did everything she could to win Peter over. And she succeeded.

Dear Kitty,

This is the first Saturday in months that hasn't been tiresome, dreary and boring. The reason is Peter. This morning as I was on my way to the attic to hang up my apron, Father asked whether I wanted to stay and practise my French, and I said yes. We spoke French together for a while and I explained something to Peter, and then we worked on our English. Father read aloud from Dickens, and I was in seventh heaven, since I was sitting on Father's chair, close to Peter.

I went downstairs at quarter to eleven. When I went back up at eleven thirty, Peter was already waiting for me on the stairs. We talked until quarter to one. Whenever I leave the room, for example after a meal, and Peter has a chance and no one else can hear, he says, 'Cheerio, Anne, see you later.'

Oh, I'm so happy! I wonder if he's going to fall in love with me after all? In any case, he's a nice boy, and you have no idea how good it is to talk to him!

Mrs van D. thinks it's all right for me to talk

to Peter, but today she asked me teasingly, 'Can I trust you two up there?'

'Of course,' I protested. 'I take that as an insult!' Morning, noon and night, I look forward to seeing Peter.

Yours, Anne M. Frank

PS. Before I forget, last night everything was blanketed in snow. Now it's thawed and there's almost nothing left.

TUESDAY, 7 MARCH 1944

Dearest Kitty,

When I think back to my life in 1942, it all seems so unreal. The Anne Frank who enjoyed that heavenly existence was completely different from the one who has grown wise within these walls. Yes, it was heavenly. Five admirers on every street corner, twenty or so friends, the favourite of most of my teachers, spoiled rotten by Father and Mother, bags full of sweets and loads of pocket money. What more could anyone ask for?

You're probably wondering how I could have charmed all those people. Peter says it's because I'm 'attractive', but that isn't it entirely. The teachers were amused and entertained by my clever answers, my witty remarks, my smiling face and my critical mind. That's all I was: a terrible flirt, coquettish and amusing. I had a few plus points, which kept me in everybody's good graces: I was hard-working, honest and generous. I would never have refused anyone who wanted to peek at my answers, I was magnanimous with my sweets, and I wasn't stuck-up.

Would all that admiration eventually have made me over-confident? It's a good thing that, at the height of my glory, I was suddenly plunged into reality. It took me more than a year to get used to doing without admiration.

How did they see me at school? As the class comedian, the eternal ringleader, never in a bad mood, never a crybaby. Was it any wonder that everyone wanted to cycle to school with me or do me little favours?

I look back at that Anne Frank as a pleasant, amusing, but superficial girl, who has nothing to do with me. What did Peter say about me? 'Whenever I saw you, you were surrounded by a flock of girls and at least two boys, you were always laughing, and you were always the centre of attention!' He was right.

What's remained of that Anne Frank? Oh, I haven't forgotten how to laugh or toss off a remark, I'm just as good, if not better, at hauling people over the coals, and I can still flirt and be amusing, if I want to be . . .

But there's the catch. I'd like to live that seemingly carefree and happy life for an evening, a few days, a week. At the end of that week I'd be exhausted, and would be grateful to the first person to talk to me about something meaningful. I want friends, not admirers. People who respect me for my character and my deeds, not my flattering smile. The circle around me would be much smaller, but what does that matter, as long as they're sincere?

In spite of everything, I wasn't altogether happy in 1942; I often felt I'd been deserted, but because I was on the go all day long, I didn't think about it. I enjoyed myself as much as I could, trying consciously or unconsciously to fill the void with jokes.

Looking back, I realize that this period of my life has irrevocably come to a close; my happy-go-lucky, carefree schooldays are gone for ever. I don't even miss them. I've outgrown them. I can no longer just be frivolous, since my serious side is always there.

I see my life up till New Year 1944 as if I were looking through a powerful magnifying glass. When I was at home, my life was filled with sunshine. Then, in the middle of 1942, everything changed overnight. The quarrels, the accusations – I couldn't take it all in. I was caught off guard, and the only way I knew how to keep my bearings was to talk back.

The first half of 1943 brought crying spells, loneliness and the gradual realization of my faults and shortcomings, which were numerous and seemed even more so. I filled the day with chatter, tried to draw Pim closer to me and failed. This left me on my own to face the difficult task of improving myself so I wouldn't have to hear their reproaches, because they made me so despondent.

The second half of the year was slightly better. I became a teenager, and was treated more like a grown-up. I began to think about things and to write stories, finally coming to the conclusion that the others no longer had anything to do with me. They had no right to swing me back and forth like a pendulum on a clock. I wanted to change myself in my own way. I realized I could manage without my mother, completely and totally, and that hurt. But what affected me even more was the realization that I was never going to be able to confide in Father. I didn't trust anyone but myself.

After New Year the second big change occurred: my dream, through which I discovered my longing for ... a boy; not for a girlfriend, but for a boyfriend. I also discovered an inner happiness underneath my superficial and cheerful exterior. From time to time I was quiet. Now I live only for Peter, since what happens to me in the future depends largely on him!

I lie in bed at night, after ending my prayers with the words '*Ich danke dir für all das Gute und Liebe und Schöne*',* and I'm filled with joy. I think of going into hiding, my health and my whole being as *das Gute*; Peter's love (which is still so new and fragile and which neither of us dares to say aloud), the future, happiness and

---

* Thank you, God, for all that is good and dear and beautiful

love as *das Liebe*; the world, nature and the tremendous beauty of everything, all that splendour, as *das Schöne*.

At such moments I don't think about all the misery, but about the beauty that still remains. This is where Mother and I differ greatly. Her advice in the face of melancholy is: 'Think about all the suffering in the world and be thankful you're not part of it.' My advice is: 'Go outside, to the country, enjoy the sun and all nature has to offer. Go outside and try to recapture the happiness within yourself; think of all the beauty in yourself and in everything around you and be happy.'

I don't think Mother's advice can be right, because what are you supposed to do if you become part of the suffering? You'd be completely lost. On the contrary, beauty remains, even in misfortune. If you just look for it, you discover more and more happiness and regain your balance. A person who's happy will make others happy; a person who has courage and faith will never die in misery!

Yours, Anne M. Frank

Dearest Kitty,

It might be amusing for you (though not for me) to hear what we're going to eat today. The cleaning lady is working downstairs, so at the moment I'm seated at the van Daans' oilcloth-covered table with a handkerchief sprinkled with fragrant pre-war perfume pressed to my nose and mouth. You probably don't have the faintest idea what I'm talking about, so let me 'begin at the beginning'. The people who supply us with food coupons have been arrested, so we have just our five black-market ration books – no coupons, no fats and oils. Since Miep and Mr Kleiman are ill again, Bep can't manage the shopping. The food is wretched, and so are we. As of tomorrow, we won't have a scrap of fat, butter or margarine. We can't eat fried potatoes for breakfast (which we've been doing to save on bread), so we're having porridge instead, and because Mrs van D. thinks we're starving, we bought some milk and some cream. Lunch today consists of mashed potatoes and pickled kale. This explains the precautionary measure with the handkerchief. You wouldn't believe how much kale can stink when it's a few years old! The kitchen smells like a mixture of spoiled plums, rotten eggs and brine. Ugh, just the thought of having to eat that muck makes me want to be sick! Besides that, our potatoes have contracted such strange diseases that one out of every two buckets of *pommes de terre* ends up in the dustbin. We entertain ourselves by trying to work out which disease they've got, and we've reached the conclusion that they suffer from cancer, smallpox and measles. Honestly, being in hiding during the fourth year of the war is no picnic. If only the whole stinking mess were over!

To tell you the truth, the food wouldn't matter so much to me if life here were more pleasant in other ways. But that's just it: this tedious existence is starting to make us all disagreeable. Here are the opinions of the five grown-ups on the present situation (children aren't allowed to have opinions, and for once I'm sticking to the rules):

Mrs van Daan: 'I'd stopped wanting to be queen of the kitchen long ago. But sitting around doing nothing was boring, so I went back to cooking. Still, I can't help complaining: it's impossible to cook without oil, and all those disgusting smells make me feel like retching. Besides, what do I get in return for my efforts? Ingratitude and rude remarks. I'm always the black sheep; I get blamed for everything. What's more, it's my opinion that the war is making very little progress. The Germans will win in the end. I'm terrified that we're going to starve, and when I'm in a bad mood, I snap at everyone who comes near.'

Mr van Daan: 'I just smoke and smoke and smoke. Then the food, the political situation and Kerli's moods don't seem so bad. Kerli's a sweetheart. If I don't have anything to smoke, I feel ill, then I need to eat meat, life becomes unbearable, nothing's good enough, and there's bound to be a flaming row. My Kerli's an idiot.'

Mrs Frank: 'Food's not very important, but I'd love a slice of rye bread right now, because I'm so hungry. If I were Mrs van Daan, I'd have put a stop to Mr van Daan's smoking long ago. But I desperately need a cigarette now, because my head's in such a whirl. The van Daans are horrible people; the British may make a lot of mistakes, but the war is progressing. I should keep my mouth shut and be grateful I'm not in Poland.'

Mr Frank: 'Everything's fine, I don't need a thing. Stay calm, we've got plenty of time. Just give me my potatoes, and I'll be quiet. Better set aside some of my rations for Bep. The political situation is improving, I'm extremely optimistic.'

Mr Dussel: 'I must complete the task I've set for myself, everything must be finished on time. The political situation is looking "*gut*", it's "eempossible" for us to get caught. Me, me, me . . . !'

Yours, Anne

Dearest Kitty,

Yesterday was a very important day for me. After lunch everything was as usual. At five I put on the potatoes, and Mother gave me some blood sausage to take to Peter. I didn't want to at first, but I finally went. He wouldn't accept the sausage, and I had the dreadful feeling it was still because of that argument we'd had about distrust. Suddenly I couldn't bear it a moment longer and my eyes filled with tears. Without another word, I returned the plate to Mother and went to the lavatory to have a good cry. Afterwards I decided to talk things out with Peter. Before dinner the four of us were helping him with a crossword puzzle, so I couldn't say anything. But as we were sitting down to eat, I whispered to him, 'Are you going to practise your shorthand tonight, Peter?'

'No,' was his reply.

'I'd like to talk to you later on.'

He agreed.

After the washing up, I went to his room and asked if he'd refused the sausage because of our last quarrel. Luckily, that wasn't the reason; he just thought it was bad manners to seem so eager. It had been very hot downstairs and my face was as red as a lobster. So after taking down some water for Margot, I went back up to get a little fresh air. For the sake of appearances, I first went and stood beside the van Daans' window before going to Peter's room. He was standing on the left side of the open window, so I went over to the right side. It's much easier to talk next to an open window in semi-darkness than in broad daylight, and I think Peter felt the same way. We told each other so much, so very much, that I can't repeat it all. But it felt good; it was the most wonderful evening I've ever had in the Annexe. I'll give you a brief description of the various subjects we touched on.

First we talked about the quarrels and how I see them in a very different light these days, and then about how we've become alienated from our parents. I told Peter about Mother and Father and Margot and myself. At one point he asked, 'You always give each other a goodnight kiss, don't you?'

'One? Dozens of them. You don't, do you?'

'No, I've never really kissed anyone.'

'Not even on your birthday?'

'Yes, on my birthday I have.'

We talked about how neither of us really trusts our parents, and how his parents love each other a great deal and wish he'd confide in them, but that he doesn't want to. How I cry my heart out in bed and he goes up to the loft and swears. How Margot and I have only recently got to know each other and yet still tell each other very little, since we're always together. We talked about every imaginable thing, about trust, feelings and ourselves. Oh, Kitty, he was just as I thought he would be.

Then we talked about the year 1942, and how different we were back then; we don't even recognize ourselves from that period. How we couldn't stand each other at first. He'd thought I was a noisy pest, and I'd quickly concluded that he was nothing special. I didn't understand why he didn't flirt with me, but now I'm glad. He also mentioned how he often used to retreat to his room. I said that my noise and exuberance and his silence were two sides of the same coin, and that I also liked peace and quiet but don't have anything for myself alone, except my diary, and that everyone would rather see the back of me, starting with Mr Dussel, and that I don't always want to sit with my parents. We discussed how glad he is that my parents have children and how glad I am that he's here. How I now understand his need to withdraw and his relationship with his parents, and how much I'd like to help him when they argue.

'But you're always a help to me!' he said.

'How?' I asked, greatly surprised.

'By being cheerful.'

That was the nicest thing he said all evening. He also told me that he didn't mind my coming to his room the way he used to; in fact, he liked it. I also told him that all of Father's and Mother's pet names were meaningless, that a kiss here and there didn't automatically lead to trust. We also talked about doing things your own way, the diary, loneliness, the difference between everyone's inner and outer selves, my mask, etc.

It was wonderful. He must have come to love me as a friend, and, for the time being, that's enough. I'm so grateful and happy, I can't find the words. I must apologize, Kitty, since my style is not up to my usual standard today. I've just written whatever came into my head!

I have the feeling that Peter and I share a secret. Whenever he looks at me with those eyes, with that smile and that wink, it's as if a light goes on inside me. I hope things will stay like this and that we'll have many, many more happy hours together.

Your grateful and happy Anne

MONDAY, 27 MARCH 1944

Dearest Kitty,

At least one long chapter on our life in hiding should be about politics, but I've been avoiding the subject, since it interests me so little. Today, however, I'll devote an entire letter to politics.

Of course, there are many different opinions on this topic, and it's not surprising to hear it frequently discussed in times of war, but ... arguing so much about politics is just plain stupid! Let them laugh, swear, make bets, grumble and do whatever they want as long as they stew in their own juice. But don't let them argue, since that only makes things worse. The people who come from outside bring us a lot of news that later proves to be untrue; however, until now our radio has never lied. Jan, Miep, Mr Kleiman, Bep and Mr Kugler go up and down in their political moods, though Jan least of all.

Here in the Annexe the mood never varies. The endless debates over the invasion, air raids, speeches, etc., etc., are accompanied by countless exclamations such as 'Eempossible!', '*Um Gottes Willen*',* 'If they're just getting started now, how long is it going to last!', 'It's going splendidly, *gut*, great!'

Optimists and pessimists – not to mention the realists – air their opinions with unflagging energy, and as with everything else, they're all certain that they have a monopoly on the truth. It annoys a certain lady that her spouse has such supreme faith in the British, and a certain husband attacks his wife because of her teasing and disparaging remarks about his beloved nation!

---

* Oh, for God's sake

And so it goes from early in the morning to late at night; the funny part is that they never get tired of it. I've discovered a trick, and the effect is overwhelming, just like pricking someone with a pin and watching them jump. Here's how it works: I start talking about politics. All it takes is a single question, a word or a sentence, and before you know it, the entire family is involved!

TUESDAY, 28 MARCH 1944

My dearest Kitty,

As much as I'd like to write more on politics, I have lots of other news to report today. First, Mother has virtually forbidden me to go up to Peter's, since, according to her, Mrs van Daan is jealous. Second, Peter's invited Margot to join us upstairs. Whether he really means it or is just saying it out of politeness, I don't know. Third, I asked Father if he thought I should take any notice of Mrs van Daan's jealousy and he said I didn't have to.

What should I do now? Mother's angry, doesn't want me going upstairs, wants me to go back to doing my homework in the room I share with Dussel. She may be jealous herself. Father doesn't begrudge us those few hours and thinks it's nice we get along so well. Margot likes Peter too, but feels that three people can't talk about the same things as two.

Father always says I'm conceited, but I'm not, I'm merely vain! I haven't had many people tell me I was pretty, except for a boy at school who said I looked so nice when I smiled. Yesterday Peter paid me a true compliment, and just for fun I'll give you a rough idea of our conversation.

Peter often says, 'Smile!' I thought it was strange, so yesterday I asked him, 'Why do you always want me to smile?'

'Because you get dimples in your cheeks. How do you do that?'

'I was born with them. There's also one in my chin. It's the only mark of beauty I possess.'

'No, no, that's not true!'

'Yes, it is. I know I'm not beautiful. I never have been and I never will be!'

'I don't agree. I think you're pretty.'

'I am not.'

'I say you are, and you'll have to take my word for it!'

So of course I then said the same about him.

Yours, Anne M. Frank

The Dutch government (in exile in London) said that, after the war, diaries and letters by forced labourers should be made public in order to put on record the suffering of the ordinary Dutch people living under the German occupation. Everybody in the Annexe knew that Anne was keeping a diary, even though they had never read it. They told her that perhaps her diary would be published, too. Anne thought it might be an interesting idea to write a novel about the Annexe. She would call it simply *The Annexe* – the title alone would make people think it was a detective story.

'Seriously, though,' she wrote, 'ten years after the war people would find it very amusing to read how we lived, what we ate and what we talked about as Jews in hiding.'

MONDAY, 3 APRIL 1944

My dearest Kitty,

Contrary to my usual practice, I'm going to write you a detailed description of the food situation, since it's become a matter of some difficulty and importance, not only here in the Annexe, but in all of Holland, all of Europe and even beyond.

In the twenty-one months we've lived here, we've been through a good many 'food cycles' – you'll understand what that means in a moment. A 'food cycle' is a period in which we have only one particular dish or type of vegetable to eat. For a long time we ate nothing but endive. Endive with sand, endive without sand, endive with mashed potatoes, endive and mashed potato casserole. Then it was spinach, followed by kohlrabi, salsify, cucumbers, tomatoes, sauerkraut, etc., etc.

It's not much fun when you have to eat, say, sauerkraut every day for lunch and dinner, but when you're hungry enough, you do a lot of things. Now, however, we're going through the most delightful period so far, because there are no vegetables at all.

Our weekly lunch menu consists of brown beans, split-pea soup, potatoes with dumplings, potato kugel and, by the grace of God, turnip tops or rotten carrots, and then it's back to brown beans. Because of the bread shortage, we eat potatoes at every meal, starting with break-fast, but then we fry them a little. To make soup we use brown beans, haricot beans, potatoes, packets of vegetable soup, packets of chicken soup and packets of bean soup. There are brown beans in everything, including the bread. For dinner we always have potatoes with imitation gravy and – thank goodness we've still got it – beetroot salad. I must tell you about the dump-lings. We make them with government-issue flour, water and yeast. They're so gluey and tough that it feels as if you have rocks in your stomach, but oh well!

The high point is our weekly slice of liver sausage, and the jam on our unbuttered bread. But we're still alive, and much of the time it still tastes good too!

Yours, Anne M. Frank

While her living space was confined to a few square metres, Anne created a whole world for herself out of nothing really, because nothing much actually happened in the Annexe. But right there, in that very small space, Anne developed into a writer. Writing became a substitute for everything – the friends, the life she was denied by the circumstances of her existence. In her diary entry for Wednesday, 5 April 1944, she put it this way:

When I write I can shake off all my cares. My sorrow disappears, my spirits are revived! But, and that's a big question, will I ever be able to write something great, will I ever become a journalist or a writer?

I hope so, oh, I hope so very much, because writing allows me to record everything, all my thoughts, ideals and fantasies.

Another break-in caused great upset. Luckily, once again the people in the Annexe were not discovered. It was decided, however, to take stricter precautions, as Anne wrote in her diary entry for Tuesday, 11 April 1944:

This incident has brought about a whole lot of changes. As of now, Dussel will be doing his work in the bathroom, and Peter will be patrolling the house between eight thirty and nine thirty. Peter isn't allowed to open his window any more, since one of the Keg people noticed it was open. We can no longer flush the toilet after nine thirty at night. Mr Sleegers has been hired as night watchman, and tonight a carpenter from the underground is coming to make a barricade out of our white Frankfurt bedsteads. Debates are going on left and right in the Annexe. Mr Kugler has reproached us for our carelessness. Jan also said we should never go downstairs. What we have to do now is find out whether Sleegers can be trusted, whether the dogs will bark if they hear someone behind the door, how to make the barricade, all sorts of things.

We've been strongly reminded of the fact that we're Jews in chains, chained to one spot, without any rights, but with a thousand obligations. We must put our feelings aside; we must be brave and strong, bear discomfort without complaint, do whatever is in our power and trust in God. One day this terrible war will be over. The time will come when we'll be people again and not just Jews!

Who has inflicted this on us? Who has set us

apart from all the rest? Who has put us through such suffering? It's God who has made us the way we are, but it's also God who will lift us up again. In the eyes of the world, we're doomed, but if, after all this suffering, there are still Jews left, the Jewish people will be held up as an example. Who knows, maybe our religion will teach the world and all the people in it about goodness, and that's the reason, the only reason, we have to suffer. We can never be just Dutch, or just English, or whatever, we will always be Jews as well. And we'll have to keep on being Jews, but then, we'll want to be.

Be brave! Let's remember our duty and perform it without complaint. There will be a way out. God has never deserted our people. Through the ages Jews have had to suffer, but through the ages they've gone on living, and the centuries of suffering have only made them stronger. The weak shall fall and the strong shall survive and not be defeated!

That night I really thought I was going to die. I waited for the police and I was ready for death, like a soldier on a battlefield. I'd gladly have given my life for my country. But now, now that I've been spared, my first wish after the war is to become a Dutch citizen. I love the Dutch, I love this country, I love the language, and I want to work here. And even if I have to write to the Queen herself, I won't give up until I've reached my goal!

I'm becoming more and more independent of my parents. Young as I am, I face life with more courage and have a better and truer sense of justice than Mother. I know what I want, I have a goal, I have opinions, a religion and love. If only I can be myself, I'll be satisfied. I know that I'm a woman, a woman with inner strength and a great deal of courage!

If God lets me live, I'll achieve more than Mother ever did, I'll make my voice heard, I'll go out into the world and work for mankind!

I now know that courage and happiness are needed first!

Yours, Anne M. Frank

Dearest Kitty,

First the weekly news! We're having a break from politics. There's nothing, and I mean absolutely nothing, to report. I'm also gradually starting to believe that the invasion will come. After all, they can't let the Russians do all the dirty work; actually, the Russians aren't doing anything at the moment either.

Mr Kleiman comes to the office every morning now. He got a new set of springs for Peter's divan, so Peter will have to get to work reupholstering it. Not surprisingly, he isn't at all in the mood. Mr Kleiman also brought some flea powder for the cats.

Have I told you that our Boche has disappeared? We haven't seen hide nor hair of her since last Thursday. She's probably already in cat heaven, while some animal lover has turned her into a tasty dish. Perhaps some girl who can afford it will be wearing a cap made of Boche's fur. Peter is heartbroken.

For the last two weeks we've been eating lunch at eleven thirty on Saturdays; in the mornings we have to make do with a cup of porridge.

Starting tomorrow it'll be like this every day; that saves us a meal. Vegetables are still very hard to come by. This afternoon we had rotten boiled lettuce. Ordinary lettuce, spinach and boiled lettuce, that's all there is. Add to that rotten potatoes, and you have a meal fit for a king!

I hadn't had my period for more than two months, but it finally started last Sunday. Despite the mess and bother, I'm glad it hasn't deserted me.

As you can no doubt imagine, we often say in despair, 'What's the point of the war? Why, oh, why can't people live together peacefully? Why all this destruction?'

The question is understandable, but so far no one has come up with a satisfactory answer. Why is England manufacturing bigger and better aeroplanes and bombs and at the same time churning out new houses for reconstruction? Why are millions spent on the war each day, while not a penny is available for medical science, artists or the poor? Why do people have to starve when mountains of food are rotting away in other parts of the world? Oh, why are people so crazy?

I don't believe the war is simply the work of politicians and capitalists. Oh no, the common man is every bit as guilty; otherwise, people and nations would have rebelled long ago! There's a destructive urge in people, the urge to rage, murder and kill. And until all of humanity, without exception, undergoes a metamorphosis, wars will continue to be waged, and everything that has been carefully built up, cultivated and grown will be cut down and destroyed, only to start all over again!

I've often been down in the dumps, but never desperate. I look upon our life in hiding as an interesting adventure, full of danger and romance, and every privation as an amusing addition to my diary. I've made up my mind to lead a different life from other girls, and not to become an ordinary housewife later on. What I'm experiencing here is a good beginning to an interesting life, and that's the reason – the only reason – why I have to laugh at the humorous side of the most dangerous moments.

I'm young and have many hidden qualities; I'm young and strong and living through a big adventure; I'm right in the middle of it and can't spend all day complaining because it's impossible to have any fun! I'm blessed with many things: happiness, a cheerful disposition and strength. Every day I feel myself maturing, I feel liberation drawing near, I feel the beauty of nature and the goodness of the people around me. Every day I think what a fascinating and amusing adventure this is! With all that, why should I despair?

Yours, Anne M. Frank

MONDAY, 8 MAY 1944

Dearest Kitty,

Have I ever told you anything about our family? I don't think I have, so let me begin. Father was born in Frankfurt am Main to very wealthy parents: Michael Frank owned a bank and became a millionaire, and Alice Stern's parents were prominent and well-to-do. Michael Frank didn't start out rich; he was a self-made man. In his youth Father led the life of a rich man's son. Parties every week, balls, banquets, beautiful girls, waltzing, dinners, a huge house, etc. After Grandpa died, most of the money was lost, and after the Great War and inflation there was nothing left at all. Until the war there were still quite a few rich relatives. So Father was extremely well bred, and he had to laugh yesterday because for the first time in his fifty-five years, he scraped out the frying pan at the table.

Mother's family wasn't as wealthy, but still fairly well off, and we've listened open-mouthed to stories of private balls, dinners and engagement parties with 250 guests.

We're far from rich now, but I've pinned all my hopes on after the war. I can assure you, I'm not so set on a bourgeois life as Mother and Margot. I'd like to spend a year in Paris and London learning the languages and studying art history. Compare that with Margot, who wants to nurse newborn babies in Palestine. I still have visions of gorgeous dresses and fascinating people. As I've told you many times before, I want to see the world and do all kinds of exciting things, and a little money won't hurt!

This morning Miep told us about her cousin's engagement party, which she went to on Saturday.

The cousin's parents are rich, and the groom's are even richer. Miep made our mouths water telling us about the food that was served: vegetable soup with meatballs, cheese, meat rolls, hors d'oeuvres made with eggs and roast beef, cheese rolls, gateaus, wine and cigarettes, and you could eat as much as you wanted.

If Miep had taken us along to the party, there wouldn't have been any rolls left over for the other guests. If we'd been there, we'd have snatched up everything in sight, including the furniture. I tell you, we were practically pulling the words right out of her mouth. We were gathered around her as if we'd never in all our lives heard of delicious food or elegant people! And these are the granddaughters of the distinguished millionaire. The world is a crazy place!

Yours, Anne M. Frank

WEDNESDAY, 10 MAY 1944

Dearest Kitty,

We were sitting in the attic yesterday afternoon working on our French when suddenly I heard the splatter of water behind me. I asked Peter what it might be. Without pausing to reply, he dashed up to the loft – the scene of the disaster – and shoved Mouschi, who was squatting beside her soggy litter box, back to the right place. This was followed by shouts and squeals, and then Mouschi, who by that time had finished peeing, took off downstairs. In search of something similar to her box, Mouschi had found herself a pile of wood shavings, right over a crack in the floor. The puddle immediately trickled down to the attic and, as luck would have it, landed in and next to the potato barrel. The ceiling was dripping, and since the attic floor has also got its share of cracks, little yellow drops were leaking through the ceiling and on to the dining table, between a pile of stockings and books.

I was doubled up with laughter, it was such a funny sight. There was Mouschi crouched under a chair, Peter armed with water, powdered bleach and a cloth, and Mr van Daan trying to calm everyone down. The room was soon set to rights, but it's a well-known fact that cat puddles stink to high heaven. The potatoes proved that all too well, as did the wood shavings, which

Father collected in a bucket and brought downstairs to burn.

Poor Mouschi! How were you to know it's impossible to get peat for your box?

Anne

THURSDAY, 11 MAY 1944

Dearest Kitty,

A new sketch to make you laugh:

Peter's hair had to be cut, and as usual his mother was to be the hairdresser. At seven twenty-five Peter vanished into his room, and reappeared on the stroke of seven thirty, stripped down to his blue swimming trunks and a pair of gym shoes.

'Are you coming?' he asked his mother.

'Yes, I'll be up in a minute, but I can't find the scissors!'

Peter helped her look, rummaging around in her cosmetics drawer. 'Don't make such a mess, Peter,' she grumbled.

I didn't catch Peter's reply, but it must have been insolent, because she cuffed him on the arm. He cuffed her back, she punched him with all her might, and Peter pulled his arm away with a look of mock horror on his face. 'Come on, old girl!'

Mrs van D. stayed put. Peter grabbed her by the wrists and pulled her all around the room. She laughed, cried, scolded and kicked, but nothing helped. Peter led his prisoner as far as the attic stairs, where he was obliged to let go of her. Mrs van D. came back to the room and collapsed into a chair with a loud sigh.

'*Die Entführung der Mutter*,'* I joked.

'Yes, but he hurt me.'

I went to have a look and cooled her hot, red wrists with water. Peter, still by the stairs and growing impatient again, strode into the room with his belt in his hand, like a lion tamer. Mrs van D. didn't move, but stayed by her writing desk, looking for a handkerchief. 'You've got to apologize first.'

'All right, I hereby offer my apologies, but only because if I don't, we'll be here till midnight.'

Mrs van D. had to laugh in spite of herself. She got up and went towards the door, where

---

* *The Abduction of Mother*, a possible reference to Mozart's opera *The Abduction from the Seraglio*

she felt obliged to give us an explanation. (By 'us' I mean Father, Mother and me; we were busy washing up.) 'He wasn't like this at home,' she said. 'I'd have belted him so hard he'd have gone flying down the stairs [!]. He's never been so insolent. This isn't the first time he's deserved a good hiding. That's what you get with a modern upbringing, modern children. I'd never have grabbed my mother like that. Did you treat your mother that way, Mr Frank?' She was very upset, pacing back and forth, saying whatever came into her head, and she still hadn't gone upstairs. Finally, at long last, she made her exit.

Less than five minutes later she stormed back down the stairs, with her cheeks all puffed out, and flung her apron on a chair. When I asked if she was through, she replied that she was going downstairs. She tore down the stairs like a tornado, probably straight into the arms of her Putti.

She didn't come up again until eight, this time with her husband. Peter was dragged from the attic, given a merciless scolding and showered with abuse: ill-mannered good-for-nothing brat, bad example, Anne this, Margot that, I couldn't hear the rest.

Everything seems to have calmed down again today!

Yours, Anne M. Frank

TUESDAY, 16 MAY 1944

My dearest Kitty,

Just for a change (since we haven't had one of these in so long) I'll recount a little discussion between Mr and Mrs van D. last night:

Mrs van D.: 'The Germans have had plenty of time to fortify the Atlantic Wall, and they'll certainly do everything within their power to hold back the British. It's amazing how strong the Germans are!'

Mr van D.: 'Oh, yes, amazing!'

Mrs van D.: 'It is!'

Mr van D.: 'So strong they're bound to win the war in the end, is that what you mean?'

Mrs van D.: 'They might. I'm not convinced that they won't.'

Mr van D.: 'I won't even answer that.'

Mrs van D.: 'You always end up answering.

You let yourself get carried away, every single time.'

Mr van D.: 'No, I don't. I always keep my answers to the bare minimum.'

Mrs van D.: 'But you always do have an answer and you always have to be right! Your predictions hardly ever come true, you know!'

Mr van D.: 'So far they have.'

Mrs van D.: 'No they haven't. You said the invasion was going to start last year, the Finns were supposed to have been out of the war by now, the Italian campaign ought to have been over by last winter, and the Russians should already have captured Lemberg. Oh no, I don't set much store by your predictions.'

Mr van D. (leaping to his feet): 'Why don't you shut your trap for a change? I'll show you who's right; some day you'll get tired of needling me. I can't stand your bellyaching a minute longer. Just wait, one day I'll make you eat your words!' (End of Act One.)

Actually, I couldn't help giggling. Mother couldn't either, and even Peter was biting his lips to keep from laughing. Oh, those stupid grown-ups. They need to learn a few things first before they start making so many remarks about the younger generation!

Since Friday we've been keeping the windows open again at night.

Yours, Anne M. Frank

What Our Annexe Family Is Interested In (A Systematic Survey of Courses and Reading Matter)

Mr van Daan: No courses; looks up many things in Knaur's *Encyclopedia and Lexicon*; likes to read detective stories, medical books and love stories, exciting or trivial.

Mrs van Daan: A correspondence course in English; likes to read biographical novels and occasionally other kinds of novels.

Mr Frank: Is learning English (Dickens!) and a bit of Latin; never reads novels, but likes serious, rather dry descriptions of people and places.

Mrs Frank: A correspondence course in English; reads everything except detective stories.

Mr Dussel: Is learning English, Spanish and Dutch with no noticeable results; reads everything; goes along with the opinion of the majority.

Peter van Daan: Is learning English, French (correspondence course), shorthand in Dutch, English and German, commercial correspondence in English, woodworking, economics and sometimes maths; seldom reads, sometimes geography.

Margot Frank: Correspondence courses in English, French and Latin, shorthand in English, German and Dutch, trigonometry, solid geometry, mechanics, physics, chemistry, algebra, geometry, English literature, French literature, German literature, Dutch literature, bookkeeping, geography, modern history, biology, economics; reads everything, preferably on religion and medicine.

Anne Frank: Shorthand in French, English, German and Dutch, geometry, algebra, history, geography, art history, mythology, biology, Bible history, Dutch literature; likes to read biographies, dull or exciting, and history books (sometimes novels and light reading).

Dearest Kitty,

I felt rotten yesterday. Throwing up (me of all people!), headache, stomach ache and anything else you can imagine. I'm feeling better today. I'm famished, but I think I'll skip the beans we're having for dinner.

Everything's going fine between Peter and me. The poor boy has an even greater need for tenderness than I do. He still blushes every evening when he gets his goodnight kiss, and then begs for another one. Am I merely a better substitute for Boche? I don't mind. He's so happy just knowing somebody loves him.

After my laborious conquest, I've distanced myself a little from the situation, but you mustn't think my love has cooled. Peter's a sweetheart, but I've slammed the door to my inner self; if he ever wants to force the lock again, he'll have to use a harder crowbar!

Yours, Anne M. Frank

Dearest Kitty,

Last night when I came down from the attic, I noticed, the moment I entered the room, that the lovely vase of carnations had fallen over. Mother was down on her hands and knees mopping up the water and Margot was fishing my papers from off the floor. 'What happened?' I asked with anxious foreboding, and before they could reply, I assessed the damage from across the room. My entire genealogy folder, my exercise books, my textbooks, everything was afloat. I nearly cried, and I was so upset I started speaking German. I can't remember a word, but according to Margot I babbled something about *'unübersehbarer Schaden, schrecklich, entsetzlich, nie zu ersetzen'** and much more. Father burst out laughing and Mother and Margot joined in, but I felt like crying because all my work and elaborate notes were lost.

I took a closer look and, luckily, the 'incalculable loss' wasn't as bad as I'd expected. Up in the attic I carefully peeled apart the sheets of

---

* Incalculable loss, terrible, awful, irreplaceable

paper that were stuck together and then hung them on the clothes line to dry. It was such a funny sight, even I had to laugh. Maria de' Medici alongside Charles V, William of Orange and Marie Antoinette.

'It's *Rassenschande*,'* Mr van Daan joked.

After entrusting my papers to Peter's care, I went back downstairs.

'Which books are ruined?' I asked Margot, who was going through them.

'Algebra,' Margot said.

But as luck would have it, my algebra book wasn't entirely ruined. I wish it had fallen right in the vase. I've never loathed any book as much as that one. Inside the front cover are the names of at least twenty girls who had it before I did. It's old, yellowed, full of scribbles, crossed-out words and revisions. The next time I'm in a wicked mood, I'm going to tear the flaming thing to pieces!

Yours, Anne M. Frank

Anne's inner turmoil showed time and time again. She liked to laugh and enjoyed amusing situations, but it was

---

* An affront to racial purity

impossible to hide her deeper, melancholic side. On Friday, 26 May 1944, she wrote:

I've asked myself again and again whether it wouldn't have been better if we hadn't gone into hiding, if we were dead now and didn't have to go through this misery, especially so that the others could be spared the burden. But we all shrink from this thought. We still love life, we haven't yet forgotten the voice of nature, and we keep hoping, hoping for ... everything.

Let something happen soon, even an air raid. Nothing can be more crushing than this anxiety. Let the end come, however cruel; at least then we'll know whether we are to be the victors or the vanquished.

FRIDAY, 2 JUNE 1944

Dear Kitty,

'If you're going to the attic, take an umbrella with you, preferably a large one!' This is to protect you from 'household showers'. There's a Dutch proverb: 'High and dry, safe and sound', but it obviously doesn't apply to wartime (guns!) and to people in hiding (litter box!). Mouschi's got into the habit of relieving herself on some newspapers or between the cracks in the floorboards, so we have good reason to fear the splatters and, even worse, the stench. The new Moortje in the warehouse has the same problem. Anyone who's ever had a cat that's not house-broken can imagine the smells, other than pepper and thyme, that permeate this house.

I also have a brand-new prescription for gunfire jitters: when the shooting gets loud, proceed to the nearest wooden staircase. Run up and down a few times, making sure to stumble at least once. What with the scratches and the noise of running and falling, you won't even be able to hear the shooting, much less worry about it. Yours truly has put this magic formula to use, with great success!

Yours, Anne M. Frank

TUESDAY, 6 JUNE 1944

My dearest Kitty,
'This is D-Day,' the BBC announced at twelve. 'This is the day.' The invasion has begun!

This morning at eight the British reported heavy bombing of Calais, Boulogne, Le Havre and Cherbourg, as well as Pas de Calais (as usual). Further, as a precautionary measure for those in the occupied territories, everyone living within a zone of twenty miles from the coast was warned to prepare for bombardments. Where possible, the British will drop pamphlets an hour ahead of time.

According to the German news, British paratroopers have landed on the coast of France. 'British landing craft are engaged in combat with German naval units,' according to the BBC.

Conclusion reached by the Annexe while breakfasting at nine: this is a trial landing, like the one two years ago in Dieppe.

BBC broadcast in German, Dutch, French and other languages at ten: the invasion has begun! So this is the 'real' invasion. BBC broadcast in German at eleven: speech by Supreme Commander General Dwight Eisenhower.

BBC broadcast in English: 'This is D-Day.' General Eisenhower said to the French people: 'Stiff fighting will come now, but after this the victory. The year 1944 is the year of complete victory. Good luck!'

BBC broadcast in English at one: 11,000 planes are shuttling back and forth or standing by to land troops and bomb behind enemy lines; 4,000 landing craft and small boats are continually arriving in the area between Cherbourg and Le Havre. British and American troops are already engaged in heavy combat. Speeches by Gerbrandy, the prime minister of Belgium, King Haakon of Norway, de Gaulle of France, the King of England and, last but not least, Churchill.

A huge commotion in the Annexe! Is this really the beginning of the long-awaited liberation? The liberation we've all talked so much about, which still seems too good, too much of a fairy tale, ever to come true? Will this year, 1944, bring us victory? We don't know yet. But where there's hope, there's life. It fills us with fresh courage and makes us strong again. We'll need to be brave to endure the many fears and hardships and the suffering yet to come. It's now a matter of remaining calm and steadfast, of gritting our teeth and keeping a stiff upper lip! France, Russia, Italy, and even Germany, can cry out in agony, but we don't yet have that right!

Oh, Kitty, the best part about the invasion is that I have the feeling that friends are on the way. Those awful Germans have oppressed and threatened us for so long that the thought of friends and salvation means everything to us! Now it's not just the Jews, but Holland and all of occupied Europe. Maybe, Margot says, I can even go back to school in September or October.

Yours, Anne M. Frank

PS. I'll keep you informed of the latest news!

This morning and last night, dummies made of straw and rubber were dropped from the air behind German lines, and they exploded the minute they hit the ground. Many paratroopers, their faces blackened so they couldn't be seen in the dark, landed as well. The French coast was bombarded with 5,500 tons of bombs during the night, and then, at six in the morning, the first landing craft came ashore. Today there were 20,000 aeroplanes in action. The German coastal batteries were destroyed even before the landing; a small bridgehead has already been formed. Everything's going well, despite the bad weather. The army and the people are 'one will and one hope'.

Dearest Kit,

Another birthday has gone by, so I'm now fifteen. I received quite a few gifts: Springer's five-volume art history book, a set of underwear, two belts, a handkerchief, two pots of yoghurt, a pot of jam, two honey biscuits (small), a botany book from Father and Mother, a gold bracelet from Margot, a sticker album from the van Daans, Biomalt and sweet peas from Dussel, sweets from Miep, sweets and exercise books from Bep, and the high point: the book *Maria Theresa* and three slices of full-cream cheese from Mr Kugler. Peter gave me a lovely bouquet of peonies; the poor boy had put a lot of effort into finding a present, but nothing quite worked out.

Wishes, thoughts, accusations and reproaches are swirling around in my head. I'm not really as conceited as many people think; I know my various faults and shortcomings better than anyone else, but there's one difference: I also know that I want to change, will change and already have changed greatly!

Why is it, I often ask myself, that everyone still thinks I'm so pushy and such a know-it-all? Am I really so arrogant? Am *I* the one who's so arrogant, or are they? It sounds silly, I know, but I'm not going to cross out that last sentence, because it's not as silly as it seems. Mrs van Daan and Dussel, my two chief accusers, are known to be totally unintelligent and, not to put too fine a point on it, just plain 'stupid'! Stupid people usually can't bear it when others do something better than they do; the best examples of this are those two dunces, Mrs van Daan and Dussel. Mrs van D. thinks I'm stupid because I don't suffer so much from this ailment as she does, she thinks I'm pushy because she's even pushier, she thinks my dresses are too short because hers are even shorter, and she thinks I'm such a know-it-all because she talks twice as much as I do about topics she knows nothing about. The same goes for Dussel. But one of my favourite sayings is 'Where there's smoke there's fire', and I readily admit I'm a know-it-all.

What's so difficult about my personality is that I scold and curse myself much more than anyone else does; if Mother adds her advice, the pile of sermons becomes so thick that I despair of ever getting through them. Then I talk back and start contradicting everyone until the old familiar Anne refrain inevitably crops up again: 'No one understands me!'

This phrase is part of me, and as unlikely as it may seem, there's a kernel of truth in it. Sometimes I'm so deeply buried under self-reproaches that I long for a word of comfort to help me dig myself out again. If only I had someone who took my feelings seriously. Alas, I haven't yet found that person, so the search must go on.

I know you're wondering about Peter, aren't you, Kit? It's true, Peter loves me, not as a girlfriend, but as a friend. His affection grows day by day, but some mysterious force is holding us back, and I don't know what it is.

Sometimes I think my terrible longing for him was over-exaggerated. But that's not true, because if I'm unable to go to his room for a day or two, I long for him as desperately as I ever did. Peter is kind and good, and yet I can't deny that he's disappointed me in many ways.

I especially don't care for his dislike of religion, his talk of food and various things of that nature. Still, I'm firmly convinced that we'll stick to our agreement never to quarrel. Peter is peace-loving, tolerant and extremely easygoing. He lets me say a lot of things to him that he'd never accept from his mother. He's making a determined effort to remove the blots from his copybook and keep his affairs in order. Yet why does he hide his innermost self and never allow me access? Of course, he's much more closed than I am, but I know from experience (even though I'm constantly being accused of knowing all there is to know in theory, but not in practice) that, in time, even the most uncommunicative types will long as much, or even more, for someone to confide in.

Peter and I have both spent our contemplative years in the Annexe. We often discuss the future, the past and the present, but as I've already told you, I miss the real thing, and yet I know it exists!

Is it because I haven't been outdoors for so long that I've become so mad about nature? I remember a time when a magnificent blue sky, chirping birds, moonlight and budding blossoms wouldn't have captivated me. Things have changed since I came here. One night during Whitsun, for instance, when it was so hot, I struggled to keep my eyes open until eleven thirty so I could get a good look at the moon, all on my own for once. Alas, my sacrifice was in vain, since there was too much glare and I couldn't risk opening a window. Another time, several months ago, I happened to be upstairs one night when the window was open. I didn't go back down until it had to be closed again. The dark, rainy evening, the wind, the racing clouds had me spellbound; it was the first time in a year and a half that I'd seen the night face-to-face. After that evening my longing to see it again was even greater than my fear of burglars, a dark rat-infested house or police raids. I went downstairs all by myself and looked out of the windows in the kitchen and private office. Many people think nature is beautiful, many people sleep from time to time under the starry sky, and many people in hospitals and prisons long for the day when they'll be free to enjoy what nature has to offer. But few are as isolated and cut off as we are from the joys of nature, which can be shared by rich and poor alike.

It's not just my imagination – looking at the sky, the clouds, the moon and the stars really does make me feel calm and hopeful. It's much better medicine than valerian or bromide. Nature makes me feel humble and ready to face every blow with courage!

As luck would have it, I'm only able – except for a few rare occasions – to view nature through dusty curtains tacked over dirt-caked windows; it takes the pleasure out of looking. Nature is the one thing for which there is no substitute!

Yours, Anne M. Frank

FRIDAY, 23 JUNE 1944

Dearest Kitty,

Nothing special going on here. The British have begun their all-out attack on Cherbourg. According to Pim and Mr van Daan, we're sure to be liberated before 10 October. The Russians are taking part in the campaign; yesterday they started their offensive near Vitebsk, exactly three years to the day that the Germans invaded Russia.

Bep's spirits have sunk lower than ever. We're nearly out of potatoes; from now on, we're going to count them out for each person, then everyone can do what they want with them. Starting Monday, Miep's taking a week's holiday. Mr Kleiman's doctors haven't found anything on the X-rays. He's torn between having an operation and letting matters take their course.

Yours, Anne M. Frank

THURSDAY, 6 JULY 1944

Dearest Kitty,

My blood runs cold when Peter talks about becoming a criminal or a speculator; of course, he's joking, but I still have the feeling he's afraid of his own weakness. Margot and Peter are always saying to me, 'If I had your pluck and your strength, if I had your drive and unflagging energy, I could . . . !'

Is it really such an admirable trait not to let myself be influenced by others? Am I right in following my own conscience?

To be honest, I can't imagine how anyone could say 'I'm weak' and then stay that way. If you know that about yourself, why not fight it, why not develop your character? Their answer has always been: 'Because it's much easier not to!' This reply leaves me feeling rather discouraged. Easy? Does that mean a life of deceit and laziness is easy too? Oh no, that can't be true. It can't be true that people are so readily tempted by ease . . . and money. I've given a lot of thought to what my answer should be, to how I should get Peter to believe in himself and, most of all, to change himself for the better. I don't know whether I'm on the right track.

I've often imagined how nice it would be if someone were to confide everything to me. But now that it's reached that point, I realize how difficult it is to put yourself in someone else's shoes and find the *right* answer. Especially since 'easy' and 'money' are new and completely alien concepts to me.

Peter's beginning to lean on me and I don't want that, not under any circumstances. It's hard enough standing on your own two feet, but when you also have to remain true to your character and soul, it's harder still.

I've been drifting around at sea, have spent days searching for an effective antidote to that terrible word 'easy'. How can I make it clear to him that, while it may seem easy and wonderful, it will drag him down to the depths, to a place where he'll no longer find friends, support or beauty, so far down that he may never rise to the surface again?

We're all alive, but we don't know why or what for; we're all searching for happiness; we're all leading lives that are different and yet the same. We three have been raised in good families, we have the opportunity to get an education and make something of ourselves. We have many reasons to hope for great happiness, but ... we have to earn it. And that's something you can't achieve by taking the easy way out. Earning happiness means doing good and working, not speculating and being lazy. Laziness may *look* inviting, but only work gives you *true* satisfaction.

I can't understand people who don't like to work, but that isn't Peter's problem either. He just doesn't have a goal, plus he thinks he's too stupid and inferior to ever achieve anything. Poor boy, he's never known how it feels to make someone else happy, and I'm afraid I can't teach him. He isn't religious, scoffs at Jesus Christ and takes the Lord's name in vain, and though I'm not Orthodox either, it hurts me every time to see him so lonely, so scornful, so wretched.

People who are religious should be glad, since not everyone is blessed with the ability to believe in a higher order. You don't even have to live in fear of eternal punishment; the concepts of purgatory, heaven and hell are difficult for many people to accept, yet religion itself, any religion, keeps a person on the right path. Not the fear of God, but upholding your own sense of honour and obeying your own conscience. How noble and good everyone could be if, at the end of each day, they were to review their own behaviour and weigh up the rights and wrongs. They would automatically try to do better at the start of each new day and, after a while, would certainly accomplish a great deal. Everyone is welcome to this prescription; it costs nothing and is definitely useful. Those who don't know will have to find out by experience that 'a quiet conscience gives you strength'!

Yours, Anne M. Frank

Dearest Kitty,

I'm finally getting optimistic. Now, at last, things are going well! They really are! Great news! An assassination attempt has been made on Hitler's life, and for once not by Jewish Communists or British capitalists, but by a German general who's not only a count, but young as well. The Führer owes his life to 'Divine Providence': he escaped, unfortunately, with only a few minor burns and scratches. A number of the officers and generals who were nearby were killed or wounded. The head of the conspiracy has been shot.

This is the best proof we've had so far that many officers and generals are fed up with the war and would like to see Hitler sink into a bottomless pit, so they can establish a military dictatorship, make peace with the Allies, rearm themselves and, after a few decades, start a new war. Perhaps Providence is deliberately biding its time getting rid of Hitler, since it's much easier, and cheaper, for the Allies to let the impeccable Germans kill each other off. It's less work for the Russians and the British, and it allows them to start rebuilding their own cities that much sooner. But we haven't reached that point yet, and I'd hate to anticipate the glorious event. Still, you've probably noticed that I'm telling the truth, the whole truth and nothing but the truth. For once, I'm not rattling on about high ideals.

Furthermore, Hitler has been so kind as to announce to his loyal, devoted people that as of today all military personnel are under orders of the Gestapo, and that any soldier who knows that one of his superiors was involved in this cowardly attempt on the Führer's life may shoot him on sight!

A fine kettle of fish that will be. Little Johnny's feet are sore after a long march and his commanding officer yells at him. Johnny grabs his rifle, shouts, 'You, you tried to kill the Führer. Take that!' One shot, and the snooty officer who dared to reprimand him passes into eternal life (or is it eternal death?). Eventually, every time an officer sees a soldier or gives an order, he'll be practically wetting his pants, because the soldiers have more say-so than he does.

Were you able to follow that, or have I been skipping from one subject to another again? I can't help it, the prospect of going back to school in October is making me too happy to be logical! Oh dear, didn't I just tell you I didn't want to anticipate events? Forgive me, Kitty, they don't call me a bundle of contradictions for nothing!

Yours, Anne M. Frank

TUESDAY, 1 AUGUST 1944

Dearest Kitty,

'A bundle of contradictions' was the end of my previous letter and is the beginning of this one. Can you please tell me exactly what 'a bundle of contradictions' is? What does 'contradiction' mean? Like so many words, it can be interpreted in two ways: a contradiction imposed from without and one imposed from within. The former means not accepting other people's opinions, always knowing best, having the last word; in short, all those unpleasant traits for which

I'm known. The latter, for which I'm not known, is my own secret.

As I've told you many times, I'm split in two. One side contains my exuberant cheerfulness, my flippancy, my joy in life and, above all, my ability to appreciate the lighter side of things. By that I mean not finding anything wrong with flirtations, a kiss, an embrace, a saucy joke. This side of me is usually lying in wait to ambush the other one, which is much purer, deeper and finer. No one knows Anne's better side, and that's why most people can't stand me. Oh, I can be an amusing clown for an afternoon, but after that everyone's had enough of me to last a month. Actually, I'm what a romantic film is to a profound thinker – a mere diversion, a comic interlude, something that is soon forgotten: not bad, but not particularly good either. I hate having to tell you this, but why shouldn't I admit it when I know it's true? My lighter, more superficial side will always steal a march on the deeper side and therefore always win. You can't imagine how often I've tried to push away this Anne, which is only half of what is known as Anne – to beat her down, hide her. But it doesn't work, and I know why.

I'm afraid that people who know me as I usually am will discover I have another side, a better and finer side. I'm afraid they'll mock me, think I'm ridiculous and sentimental and not take me seriously. I'm used to not being taken seriously, but only the 'light-hearted' Anne is used to it and can put up with it; the 'deeper' Anne is too weak. If I force the good Anne into the spotlight for even fifteen minutes, she shuts up like a clam the moment she's called upon to speak, and lets Anne number one do the talking. Before I realize it, she's disappeared.

So the nice Anne is never seen in company. She's never made a single appearance, though she almost always takes the stage when I'm alone. I know exactly how I'd like to be, how I am ... on the inside. But unfortunately I'm only like that with myself. And perhaps that's why – no, I'm sure that's the reason why – I think of myself as happy on the inside and other people think I'm happy on the outside. I'm guided by the pure Anne within, but on the outside I'm nothing but a frolicsome little goat tugging at its tether.

As I've told you, what I say is not what I feel, which is why I have a reputation for being a boy-chaser, a flirt, a smart alec and a reader of romances. The happy-go-lucky Anne laughs, gives a flippant reply, shrugs her shoulders and pretends she couldn't care less. The quiet Anne reacts in just the opposite way. If I'm being completely honest, I'll have to admit that it does matter to me, that I'm trying very hard to change myself, but that I'm always up against a more powerful enemy.

A voice within me is sobbing, 'You see, that's what's become of you. You're surrounded by negative opinions, dismayed looks and mocking faces, people who dislike you, and all because you don't listen to the advice of your own better half.' Believe me, I'd like to listen, but it doesn't work, because if I'm quiet and serious, everyone thinks I'm putting on a new act and I have to save myself with a joke, and then I'm not even talking about my own family, who assume I must be ill, stuff me with aspirins and sedatives, feel my neck and forehead to see if I have a temperature, ask about my bowel movements and berate me for being in a bad mood, until I just can't keep it up any more, because when everybody starts hovering over me, I get cross, then sad, and finally end up turning my heart inside out, the bad part on the outside and the good part on the inside, and keep trying to find a way to become what I'd like to be and what I could be if ... if only there were no other people in the world.

Yours, Anne M. Frank

ANNE'S DIARY ENDS HERE

Afterword

Anne's diary ends on Tuesday, 1 August 1944, but her life did not. Hopes that the war would come to an end soon were not fulfilled. On Friday, 4 August 1944, the eight people who had been in hiding in the Annexe were arrested, together with two of the helpers, Mr Kleiman and Mr Kugler, who were taken to prison. Mr Kleiman, who had suffered from a bad stomach for a long time, was soon released 'on grounds of ill health'. A few months later, Mr Kugler managed to escape when he was about to be transferred to Germany to do hard labour with other prisoners. Both Mr Kleiman and Mr Kugler survived the war.

The eight people from the Annexe were first taken to Westerbork, the transit camp for Jews in the north of Holland. In early September 1944 they were transferred to Auschwitz concentration camp in Poland, on the last train there from Westerbork.

At the end of October, Margot and Anne were then moved from Auschwitz to Bergen-Belsen concentration camp nearby. The conditions there were terrible. A typhus epidemic broke out and thousands perished, among them Margot and Anne Frank. The date of Anne's death is not known, but it was probably in March 1945, just two months before the war in Europe ended and Bergen-Belsen was liberated by the British Army.

Anne's father, Otto Frank, was the only one of the eight people hiding in the Annexe to survive the concentration camps. He returned to Amsterdam and stayed with Miep Gies and her husband. Miep gave him the pages of Anne's diary that she had kept in the office. Later, Otto moved to Switzerland, where he devoted himself to sharing the message of his daughter's diary with people all over the world.

Some Helpful Definitions

Adolf Hitler – the leader of the Nazi Party in Germany from 1933–45

The Allies – a group of countries, led by Great Britain, France, the United States and the Soviet Union, that fought together against Germany in the Second World War

anti-Semitism – hatred and hostility towards Jews

the black market – a system in which goods are sold and bought illegally, especially during times of rationing

the 'Brownshirts' – gangs that went around terrorizing people who did not like the Nazis; known as the 'Brownshirts' because of the colour of their uniform

capitulation – when one country surrenders to another country after an invasion

concentration camps – heavily guarded prison camps that held large numbers of prisoners 'concentrated' in small areas. Jews, and other people from different religious and ethnic backgrounds that the Nazis wanted to get rid of, were forced to do hard labour and many died of starvation and disease, or were killed by the Nazis.

D-Day – the day (6 June 1944) that the Allied forces invaded Europe

deportation – the forced removal of Jews from their homes to concentration camps

emigrate – to leave one's country to settle in another part of the world

fascists – people who supported the Italian National Fascist Party, led by the dictator Benito Mussolini during the Second World War. Like Hitler, Mussolini punished anyone who opposed his government. A fascist was also regarded as someone who used violence to force their beliefs on to others.

the Gestapo – the brutal Nazi secret state police force that spread fear and terror among people, especially the Jews; they were part of the SS

Hitler Youth – an organized youth group, founded by Hitler's Nazi Party, in which children were taught the Nazis' ideology

liberation – after Germany lost the war in 1945, the concentration camps were liberated by the Allies and the survivors were freed

Nazi Party – this was the German National Socialist Workers' Party (commonly known as the Nazi Party); led by Adolf Hitler who believed that the German people were a superior race

occupation – the control of a country by a foreign military power

pogroms – organized violence against the Jews

prejudice – pre-judging and making a decision about a person or group of people without knowing anything about them

the Resistance – Jews and non-Jews who fought back against the Nazis, including those who hid Jews; these helpers put their own lives at risk to save innocent people

the SS – the powerful Nazi security force, also known as the 'Blackshirts', that protected Hitler; they were also in charge of the concentration camps

Westerbork – the transit camp in north-east Holland, through which many thousands of Jews were deported to concentration camps in other parts of Europe. The eight people from the Secret Annexe were on the last train that left Westerbork for Auschwitz concentration camp in Poland.

yellow star – the Jewish Star of David. Hitler forced all Jews aged six and above to wear the star on their clothes so that everyone could see they were Jewish and they could be targeted for punishment or arrest.

ANNE FRANK

ABOUT THE ANNE FRANK FONDS

ANNE FRANK TRUST UK

Launched in 1991, the Anne Frank Trust UK is the British partner organization of the Anne Frank House. It is an educational charity that draws on the power of Anne Frank's life and diary to challenge prejudice and reduce hatred, encouraging people to embrace positive attitudes, responsibility and respect for others.

The trust does this through a range of travelling exhibitions and educational programmes targeted at young people, and is recognized as a leading force in the shaping of positive attitudes towards difference. It is proud to have partnered Penguin Books in several educational projects.

For more information on events and activities please email *info@annefrank.org.uk* or look at the Trust's website *www.annefrank.org.uk*

Registered charity number 1003279

ANNE FRANK
THE DIARY OF A YOUNG GIRL

THE DEFINITIVE EDITION

ANNE FRANK APP

The world's most beloved diary, brought to life in App format.

In the summer of 1942, fleeing the horrors of the Nazi occupation, Anne Frank and her family were forced into hiding in the back of an Amsterdam warehouse.

Aged thirteen when she went into the Secret Annexe, Anne kept a diary in which she confided her innermost thoughts and feelings, movingly revealing how the eight people living under these extraordinary conditions coped with the daily threat of discovery and death, with being cut off from the outside world, petty misunderstandings and the unbearable strain of living like prisoners.

Sixty-five years after it was first published by Anne's father, Otto Frank, the diary has been brought to life digitally in the Anne Frank App. Complete and unabridged, including the five 'missing pages' discovered by the Anne Frank Fonds Basel in 1998, with scores of additional images, videos and historical documents as well as audio extracts read by Helena Bonham Carter, the Anne Frank App offers unprecedented historical content. Digital readers are able to explore Anne's world: what it looked, sounded and felt like living in hiding and what, in turn, was happening outside the annexe walls.